CHEVROLET
1953
1962
1972
1·13·13
1984
1997
2005

THE SEVENTH GENERATION OF AMERICA'S SPORTS CAR

CORVETTE STINGRAY

LARRY EDSALL

motorbooks

First published in 2013 by Motorbooks, an imprint of The Quarto Group, 401 Second Avenue North, Suite 310, Minneapolis, MN 55401 USA. T (612) 344-8100 F (612) 344-8692 www.QuartoKnows.com

10 9 8 7 6 5

ISBN-13: 978-0-7603-4384-5

Library of Congress Cataloging-in-Publication Data

Edsall, Larry.
Corvette Stingray : the seventh generation of America's sports car / by Larry Edsall.
pages cm
Summary: "The definitive, GM-licensed companion book for the autumn 2013 launch of the seventh-generation Corvette, a car that continues to define and re-define the American sports car."-Provided by publisher.
Includes bibliographical references and index.
ISBN 978-0-7603-4384-5 (hc)
1. Corvette automobile. 2. Sports cars--United States--History. I. Title.
TL215.C6E37 2013
629.222'2--dc23
2013023682

Editor: Jordan Wiklund
Design Manager: Brad Springer
Cover Design: Simon Larkin
Interior Design: Brad Norr
Layout Designer: Karl Laun

On the cover: The 2014 Corvette Stingray.
On the frontis: The Corvette logo through the generations.
On the title page: At its unveiling in Detroit during the North American International Auto Show in 2013, a 2014 Corvette Stingray was suspended from the wall above the main platform.
On the back flap: An early rendition of the interior of the 2014 Corvette Stingray.
On the back cover: The first-generation Corvette (top); a computer-generated image of airflow through the 2014 Corvette in motion (left); the 2014 Corvette Stingray as it appears in Gran Turismo 5 (right).

Printed in China

CONTENTS

FOREWORD BY RON FELLOWS 6

Chapter 1 A BRIEF HISTORY OF THE CHEVROLET CORVETTE 8

Chapter 2 THE THIRD TIME REALLY IS THE CHARM 18

Chapter 3 EXTERIOR DESIGN 30

Chapter 4 INTERIOR DESIGN 52

Chapter 5 ENGINEERING DEVELOPMENTS 68

Chapter 6 THE NEW SMALL-BLOCK V-8 92

Chapter 7 ON THE ROAD, BUT UNDER CAMOUFLAGE 108

Chapter 8 LAUNCH CONTROL 134

Chapter 9 ASSEMBLY REQUIRED 152

Chapter 10 DRIVING THE DREAM 170

APPENDIX 182

SPECIFICATIONS 186

BIBLIOGRAPHY 188

ACKNOWLEDGMENTS 189

INDEX 190

DEDICATION

For Stirling Silliphant, who wrote so many of the *Route 66* television series scripts that sent Tod and Buz around the country in their Corvette and inspired my generation to want to explore the land and its people in our own cars.

FOREWORD

I'm honored and privileged to have been asked to write this foreword for the book on the new Corvette Stingray. Having been a driver with Corvette Racing through two generations of Corvettes, I've never been more excited than I am about this—the seventh-generation Corvette!

Corvette has a tremendous racing heritage, competing in long distance sports car races going back to the days of the legendary Zora Arkus-Duntov and the first-generation Corvette.

But the most successful racing generations were the C5 and C6 eras, with the birth of a factory-supported program branded Corvette Racing. Since 1999, Corvette Racing has amassed 85 victories, firmly establishing the Corvette marque as a sports car racing icon, beating the biggest names in the sports car world. And the toughest car race on the global stage is the famed 24 Hours of Le Mans—a true test of man and machine, and likely in that order! Corvette Racing, with team partner Pratt & Miller Engineering, first entered the 24 Hours of Le Mans in the year 2000. Since then, we have had seven class wins, beginning with our first Le Mans victory in 2001. It's an enviable record that any car manufacturer would love to boast of.

There is nothing like winning at Le Mans, seeing the exhausted yet proud faces of team members, and being on the top step of the podium looking out over thousands of race fans who have streamed on to the race track to surround themselves in the victory celebrations. But winning at the 24 Hours of Le Mans is far from easy. It requires incredible levels of skilled dedication and commitment, words that embody the Corvette spirit.

From our debut season in 1999, the early years of Corvette Racing were lean. We had lots to learn, on both the engineering and competition sides. But with the Corvette, we had a great baseline to work from, and putting together a passionate group of like-minded engineers and racers—focused on and dedicated to the process of winning—there was no stopping us.

We achieved Corvette Racing's first victory with the C5 in Texas on September 2, 2000. I remember like it was yesterday, mostly because the race was held in absolutely sweltering conditions! Since then, the name Corvette has been synonymous with speed and durability, the keys to winning long-distance car races.

As the fifth-generation Corvette's tenure came to a close, the C6 era began with the first opportunity for transferring long-distance racing successes to the production side of Corvette. With improved aerodynamics, lighter weight, and a more powerful and efficient six-liter V-8, the base-model Corvette was launched in 2005.

Winning definitely improves the breed. Throughout the lifespan of the C6 Corvette, the vehicle enjoyed more performance innovations and links to its racing success bloodline than any previous generation of Corvette. From the Z06 model to the ZR1, transfer of technology existed from engine performance to the use of lightweight materials and electronic driver aids—technology previously reserved for sophisticated racing applications only.

And successful partnerships in racing can play a key role on the production side as well. Michelin, for example, became a tire partner with Corvette Racing in 2004, developing race tires specific to the needs of the C6 race cars. Michelin has now developed a tire exclusive to the seventh-generation Corvette, enhancing the C7 driving experience to exhilarating new levels.

The 2014 Corvette Stingray is the culmination of 60 years of passionately dedicated designers, engineers, and racers contributing to create the most advanced, sophisticated and exciting Corvette ever. To drive a C7 is to feel in your hands and in your seat the enthusiasm and emotion of the countless people who have contributed to build the most gratifying sports car on the planet.

Enjoy this incredible inside look at what it took to develop what is unquestionably the best Corvette yet—one that is truly worthy of the Stingray name.

Ron Fellows

Corvette Racing Emeritus and Member of Corvette and Canadian Motorsports Halls of Fame

CHAPTER

1

A BRIEF OF THE CHEVROLET

Does it really matter who inspired the first Chevrolet Corvette?

Automotive design historians Michael Lamm and Dave Holls say General Motors' design chief Harley Earl was thinking of his own sons, Jim and Jerry, when he set one of his staffers to work on a small, two-seat roadster poised to become an American competitor to such European sports cars as the MG-TD and XK120 Jaguar.

Another automotive historian, Mike Mueller (as well as a display at the National Corvette Museum), says the suggestion came from Earl's friend, U.S. Air Force General Curtis LeMay. The general, who oversaw sports car races on the runways of his military bases as a way to boost morale, told Earl that an American automaker should produce a car to compete with those that many World War II veterans had brought home with them from Europe.

Yet another author/historian, David Temple, notes that in September 1951, Earl had driven from Detroit to upstate New York for the sports car races at Watkins Glen. There he led the prerace parade laps to showcase the one-of-a-kind Buick LeSabre, a jet aircraft–inspired convertible prototype GM called an "experimental laboratory on wheels." But the edge in Earl's honors at the front of the field evaporated when sportsman and racer Briggs Cunningham chided the GM design chief, because while the Buick could lead the parade, it wasn't capable of participation in the real race.

Still others have reported that Earl brought home the idea of an American-built sports car after seeing the new European models while attending early postwar auto shows in England and France.

HISTORY
CORVETTE

GM Design chief Harley Earl was teased that his LeSabre concept car was fine for leading a pre-race parade around the track, but wasn't fit for competition once the green flag flew.

A styling sketch for the original Chevrolet Corvette.

Regardless of his motivation, sometime late in 1951, Earl assigned GM designers to work on a Eurostyle two-seater. He also instructed sports car enthusiast Robert McLean to begin work on a Eurostyle two-seater that would provide the basis for an American roadster. He specified investigation into a body made not of steel or aluminum, but rather of the new composite, fiberglass-reinforced plastic material already in use for aircraft parts, boat hulls and decks, and other products, including some do-it-yourself sports car kits. Earl brought a Jaguar XK120 into the studio so his team could study the way its components were packaged on a 102-inch wheelbase. That team included Carl Renner, Henry Lauve, Duane "Sparky" Bohnstedt, and Bob McLean, a graduate of CalTech who was both an engineer and industrial designer. Automotive interior designer Joe Schemansky first imagined the Corvette's twin-cockpit interior.

By the spring of 1952, McLean's final drawings had been turned into a full-scale clay model and soon after into a fiberglass-bodied version. Chevrolet's chief engineer, Ed Cole, and general manger Thomas Keating both liked it so much that they showed it to GM president Harlow Curtice.

Curtice liked the car as well. There are reports that Earl—unwilling to leave things to chance—actually showed the car to Curtice for his preliminary approval even before sharing it with Cole and Keating. Regardless of the chronology, Cole, Keating, and Curtice liked the car and approved project EX-122, which became the car's official and internal name: EXperimental project 122, a.k.a. Project Opel. What Curtice endorsed was the construction of a show or concept car, a "dream machine" to be unveiled and featured in January 1953 in the ballroom of the Waldorf-Astoria Hotel in New York City as part of the General Motors Motorama.

In the 1930s and early 1940s, General Motors had gone to New York to show its new products to the Wall Street investment community. In 1949, GM opened its Transportation Unlimited show to the public, and more than 300,000 people came to see the new cars and to be entertained by Broadway-style musical numbers. In 1950, GM called the event the Midcentury Motorama, and once again, more than 300,000 people attended. There was no such extravaganza in 1951 or 1952, but for 1953 GM planned something very special for a new version of the Motorama—an event that would show not only the newest GM vehicles, but also a line of futuristic vehicles designed to show what might be driving down the road in the decades to come.

Engineer Maurice Olley oversaw the construction of the Project Opel sports car for the Motorama show. Ed Cole had hired him away from British luxury carmaker Rolls-Royce to lead Chevrolet's research and development efforts. Olley and his engineering team put McLean's design—with a final tweak from Clare MacKichan—atop a frame with X-shaped cross members for enhanced rigidity, crucial in a vehicle with no roof and a fiberglass (rather than metal) body structure.

While many of the car's components were salvaged from the standard Chevrolet parts bin, a modern Hotchkiss drivetrain with U-joints was created to send power to the rear wheels. Earl and McLean wanted that power to be provided by a V-8 engine borrowed from either Cadillac or Buick, but their request

The Chevrolet Corvette was unveiled in January, 1953 as part of the GM Motorama, a traveling auto show that started in New York City and then visited several other American cities.

A crowd gathers around the Chevrolet Corvette as it makes its debut in January, 1953 at the Waldorf Astoria Hotel in New York City.

was denied. Instead, power came from Chevrolet's workhorse "Blue Flame," an inline six-cylinder engine, though for the sports car the engine would be topped by a trio of carburetors and tweaked to produce 150 horsepower (42 more than in its typical application). Because of time constraints, however, that power would reach the sports car's rear wheels through a very unsporting two-speed Powerglide automatic transmission.

The car was unveiled as the Chevrolet Corvette. A French word meaning "fast sloop," a *corvette* was a small, fast-moving, highly maneuverable but powerful antisubmarine and antiaircraft warship used by the American, Canadian, and British navies during World War II. But it wasn't the car's designers who coined the vehicle's title—it was Myron Scott, a photographer in the Chevrolet public relations department.

If Cole, Olley, McLean, and the others were ever worried about what the public's reaction would be, they didn't have to sweat once Motorama was under way. The Corvette was the star of the show.

In the event the sports car was a big enough hit that General Motors would approve a production version, engineers had been working on a steel body shell. But to capitalize on the car's sudden and strong popularity (and on the futuristic appeal of the new fiberglass material), corporate officials realized they could launch production earlier by sticking with the show car's plasticized bodywork. Thus, by June 1953, the first salable Corvettes began production in a section of a Chevrolet assembly plant in Flint, Michigan.

Only 300 of those cars were built for the 1953 model year, and all were painted Polo White with red interiors. To further enhance the car's sudden fame, the 300 cars were sold only to special customers, especially to celebrities whom GM wanted the public to see driving its new sports car.

With the interest generated by the Motorama and by newspaper, magazine, and newsreel coverage of the celebrities in their Corvettes, Chevrolet anticipated American motorists would buy as many as 10,000 Corvettes (if not more) for the 1954 model year. To meet that demand, the company moved production from the makeshift assembly line in Flint to the Chevrolet assembly plant at St. Louis, Missouri.

To further accelerate interest, the company showed potential new versions of the Corvette at its Motorama show in January 1954, including a hardtop, fastback (the Corvair), and even a station wagon (the Nomad).

For 1954, the production Corvette remained an open roadster with a convertible top and removable side curtains instead of roll-up windows, although three more colors—Pennant Blue, Sportsman Red, and Black—were offered, as was a beige-toned interior.

But the demand Chevrolet had anticipated did not materialize. Only 3,640 of the 1954 cars were built, and by January 1955, a third of them still were parked in lots at the assembly plant instead of in the lots of Chevrolet dealerships or in owners' driveways.

It was an egregious oversight. There were serious discussions about removing the car from production. But then three stars unexpectedly aligned in the automotive constellation: Ford introduced a Corvette competitor, the Thunderbird; Chevrolet developed a new and compact V-8 engine; and a European-born engineer and auto racer who had been among those standing in line to see the first Corvette concept at the 1953 Motorama show convinced GM that he knew how to fulfill the company's dreams for its sports car.

That engineer and racer was Zora Arkus-Duntov, and he was hired by Ed Cole in the late spring of 1953. Before long, he had talked his way onto the Corvette engineering team. He then convinced that team to install the new V-8 engine—tuned to pump out 195 horsepower—in the car, and to link that engine to a three-speed manual transmission.

Fewer than 700 such cars were built for the 1955 model year, but with a new body design—coves sculpted into the body sides and, at last, roll-up windows—and with the V-8 engine now producing 210 horsepower, nearly 3,500 Corvettes were built for 1956. Though sales lagged behind Ford's new Thunderbird, Corvette production would nearly double for 1957, when fuel injection took the horsepower rating to 250.

THE STINGRAY MAKES WAVES

At last, the Corvette was drawing attention—not only on the street, but on the racetrack as well. In both the United States and Europe, the Corvette was turning heads during top-speed runs, veering around the curves at racing meccas such as the hard-packed sand of Daytona Beach, Florida. "Without qualification, General Motors is now building a sports car," Karl Ludvigsen reported in *Sports Car Illustrated* magazine.

Among the racing Corvettes was one specially built for Bill Mitchell, Harley Earl's longtime assistant, who at the end of 1958 inherited Earl's title and his office overlooking the two-year-old, spaceport-styled, Saarinen-designed GM Technical Center campus in Warren, Michigan, north of Detroit.

Because Mitchell enjoyed offshore fishing and his new racecar's styling—cutting through the air like a shark's fin splits water—Mitchell called his car the Stingray. With aerodynamic bodywork designed by Larry Shinoda, and driven by racer/dentist motorsport celebrity Dr. Dick Thompson, Mitchell's Stingray won on the track during the racing season, drew crowds on the auto show circuit after the season ended, and then became Mitchell's daily driver for his commute from home to the GM design studios. Life was good.

Within those studios, Mitchell's racing car—inspired by photos of Italian sports and concept cars he brought back from the Turin auto show—served as inspiration for a new and second-generation Corvette, a car launched for the 1963 model year as the Corvette Sting Ray.

For the first time, the Corvette was available as a hardtop, with a fastback-style roofline split by a feature Mitchell called the "stinger," a slight ridge that ran up through the hood, over the roof, through the window, and down to the tip of the rear deck panel. Like the riveted spine line on the famed Bugatti 57SC Atlantic (though much more subtle on the Corvette), the "split window" feature soon became an icon of automotive design, even if it was used for only a single production year.

Whether the new model was the split-window coupe (designed by Peter Brock) or the open convertible (by designer Chuck Pohlmann), not only did the new Corvette look fast, it *was* fast. Instead of the original, truck-style solid rear axle, the new Corvette had a more modern independent rear axle arrangement. To save money and space, it employed old-fashioned leaf springs mounted transversely to fit within the car's taut design. "For the first time, I now have a Corvette I can be proud to drive in Europe," Arkus-Duntov declared, before engineering a special made-for-racing version of the car called the Grand Sport.

Zora Arkus-Duntov was both an engineer and a race car driver. He's shown here in the 1957 SS, a racing version of the Chevrolet Corvette.

1
CORVETTE

CORVETTE THROUGH THE GENERATIONS

With an exciting new design available in convertible or coupe body styles, Corvette production soared to more than 20,000. By the 1968 model year, Arkus-Duntov was designated as Corvette chief engineer, and a third-generation (the so-called C3) Corvette was introduced. The C3 lacked a Sting Ray badge—after all, its styling was more shark- than ray-like—but it inspired a pair of styling concept cars known as the Mako Sharks.

Nonetheless, the Stingray designation—now one word instead of two—returned for 1969 and remained through the 1976 model year. Corvette production surpassed 40,000 units for the first time, even though production of a convertible version had ended in 1975. In 1981, Corvette production moved again, this time from St. Louis to a new assembly plant in Bowling Green, Kentucky, though for a while both facilities were building cars.

There would be no 1983 model Corvette. The equipment installation and other preparations for producing the next generation took longer than anticipated, and production of the fourth-generation Corvette (C4) wasn't launched until January 1983, for the 1984 model year.

But the car proved worth the wait. The C4 was an all-new and modern car featuring smooth, sleek lines that reduced aerodynamic drag by nearly 25 percent—an astounding number in vehicular engineering. Just as impressive was the car's movement through Chevrolet dealerships, as more than 51,000 people bought the new Corvette in the C4's first year of production.

Even though a Corvette convertible began production for 1986, sales figures declined once the initial pent-up demand was fulfilled. However, horsepower increased, with a 375-horsepower, ZR-1 version available for 1990, and then a 405-horsepower update for 1993.

A fifth-generation Corvette launched in January 1996 for 1997, though for that first model year, fewer than 10,000 were built with the new body, new-generation small-block V-8, rear-mounted transmission, and stronger, stiffer frame. The new frame was produced by an innovative hydroforming method that used water pressure to assure the uniformity and strength of the steel tubular members. By the 1998 model year, the new Corvette was available in convertible architecture as well, and production exceeded 30,000 units and remained at that level throughout the C5 production run.

C5 production ended with the 2004 model year. For 2005 there was yet another new-generation Corvette (the C6), a car that earned the Corvette supercar status in more ways than one. The base C6 pumped out 400 horsepower, and yet it could cruise down the highway sipping fuel at a rate of only one gallon per 28 miles traveled. This was high performance indeed, especially when you consider that for many Corvette owners, the car was the most fuel-efficient they owned; the other vehicle in their garages was typically a big, thirsty sport utility vehicle.

For the 2006 model year, Chevrolet introduced a 505-horsepower, Z06 version of the Corvette. Capable of achieving speeds of nearly 200 miles per hour on the test track (or the Autobahn, for more adventurous drivers), the Corvette had become a true supercar in the eyes of the world's sports car enthusiasts.

The dreams of the car's founding fathers and of all who had worked on its design and development had finally been realized. But now another realization dawned—the vision that America's sports car, *the* American sports car, might have reached the end of its road.

Bill Mitchell poses with his 1959 Stingray, a car originally built for racing but which Mitchell later used for his daily commute to the GM Design offices.

CHAPTER 2

THE THIRD REALLY IS

"We started the [Stingray] twice before."

Those words are from Tadge Juechter, the chief engineer for the seventh-generation Chevrolet Corvette, who had only months earlier feared he would become a chief engineer without portfolio.

Juechter joined the Corvette engineering team in the early 1990s and became the chief engineer for America's sports car not long after the sixth-generation Corvette was launched as a 2005 model. His team had twice begun work on a seventh-generation car, only to be halted by General Motors' financial problems. "We thought bankruptcy would mean the end of the Corvette," Juechter said. But to his very pleasant surprise, that was not the case.

It turns out, Juechter recalled, "we had friends at the Treasury Department."

In an effort to save the American automobile industry—and in turn perhaps the entire U.S. economy—the new president-elect, Barack Obama, along with several new advisors and cabinet members, created Team Auto, a group of a dozen or so financial and manufacturing experts and analysts. The team examined the state of the industry and especially the management and product plans of General Motors and Chrysler, both of which sought federal loans to stay in business. The U.S. Department of the Treasury would also play a key role in the bailout.

Among Team Auto's discoveries at General Motors was that the Chevrolet Corvette was not only profitable, but also stunningly fuel-efficient, capable of cruising along a highway at better than 25 miles per gallon. (It didn't hurt that several members of the investigative committee were Corvette fans.) Taken together, keeping the Corvette was neither a foolish (nor fuelish) idea.

TIME THE CHARM

Tadge Juechter is the chief engineer for the seventh-generation Chevrolet Corvette Stingray. He's smiling now, but he and his team suffered through two disappointing false starts on the car's development before getting the go-ahead of what was known within GM as the Y1XX project.

Harlan Charles is the product manager for the new Stingray. Though he's part of the marketing department, one of his primary roles is to serve as the voice of the customer during the car's design and development, making sure all the design elements and technological innovations enhance the driver and passenger's enjoyment of the car.

Juechter first learned of his car's reprieve while fielding questions from Team Auto about the disposition of the Bowling Green, Kentucky, assembly plant, where the Corvette was built. The first question, Juechter recalled, wasn't about justifying the operation of a plant where only one platform was produced. It wasn't even a question—it was a statement.

"Tell us about the C7."

Juechter told the committee that he and his team had started work twice on a seventh-generation Corvette. They had some ideas for improving the C6 and had begun working on them. "We're always thinking about it: if we were doing it over again, what would we do as markets change and as technology advances? What would you do differently?" Juechter asked. It was a question more for himself than anyone else, but the committee was intrigued.

"I was astonished to see the new Martian rover," he added. "It has a four megapixel camera on it. Are you kidding me? Anybody's point-and-shoot is better than that now. But," he added, "the vehicle was designed and engineered in 2004 to meet all the technical requirements at that time."

While considering such what-ifs, "we'd been charging along fat, dumb, and happy when a notice came down right before the Christmas holidays [in 2007]," he said. "We were told to stand down."

What had happened? Why was the Corvette team told to stand down? Even though the subject of a new Corvette wasn't on the budget for a high-level, future-product planning meeting at General Motors, someone at the meeting had mentioned the car and whether work should be done on a next-generation model. It was later explained to Juechter that all new projects were to cease and desist—at least for a while. "We were told to go back and figure out a way to get a few more years out of the C6," Juechter said. "After that, we got started on a less expensive, evolutionary car. But then everything stopped with the bankruptcy. Everything got canceled."

Canceled, of course, until the company emerged from bankruptcy. At that point, Juechter's team resumed its work on a C6 evolution. "We picked up the pieces where we had left off," Juechter said.

PROJECT Y1XX APPROVED

Of course, what the Corvette engineers really wanted to do was to create a new car—not something that might be considered a C6.5, but a true C7, a new and contemporary car with the latest technology and design.

To their surprise, that's just what they got to do. A seventh-generation Corvette had been approved. What came to be known within GM as Y1XX would be a true seventh-generation model.

Each time there's a next-generation Corvette, people wonder if—and some, perhaps many, enthusiasts hope—that the new car's engine will be moved from in front of to behind the cockpit, emulating so many European supercars. "Every time we do a Corvette, we talk about it, about doing a new architecture," Juechter said.

"We look at the pluses and minuses," he continued. "For us, it's not an emotional decision, although we know it is to a lot of customers. For us, it boils down to what makes the car better, and I mean *every aspect* of the car. People love the mid-engine proportions, but it is more expensive. For us, it boils down to hardcore performance measures, and to the hardcore vehicle driving experience, which includes what is it like to live with the car, to maintain it, the initial purchase price, cost of ownership, the utility of the vehicle—we've already spoiled people with the amount of luggage space in the Corvette.

"We've made a market segment–leading formula for many, many years," the chief engineer continued. "We dominate the segment two to one or more in the United States with the formula we have. We don't want to throw all that away."

The fact is, the Corvette—with its engine in front of the driver and passenger—is not only a world-class, supercar-category sports car, but also affordable to buy and to operate, with initial and operating costs only a fraction of what buyers find elsewhere, and with reliability that the makers of very few vehicles in the competitive set might ever hope to match.

Corvettes started racing as soon as the first one rolled off the assembly line, but it was the insertion of Chevrolet's small-block V-8 engine that pushed the car to the front of the field. In 1960, Corvettes raced at Le Mans, scoring their first major international victory, leading their class while finishing eighth overall.

Nonetheless, might a mid-engine Corvette be somewhere down the road? Perhaps, Juechter says. "But if we ever do go mid-engine, we will do it because we've figured out a formula that makes the whole car better."

The Corvette formula is far from secret. Though design and technology have evolved, and the car has matured and been reenergized and refined with each new generation, the Corvette DNA has remained:

- the overall proportions of its front-engine/rear-drive design, including such technical aspects as dash-to-axle effect, the spatial relationship between twinned sets of tail lamps and rear license plate, a distinct graphic element (spear or cove or gills) within the front fenders, and the way the bodywork itself seems to cascade like a waterfall between the seats in the Corvette convertible.

- the small-block V-8 engine and the way its compact dimensions (and the use of transverse rather than vertically mounted springs) enhance the driver's view of the road, a very good thing since that same small but strong engine empowers that driver to move very quickly through that field of vision.

- technological innovation and the use of advanced materials, from the original use of fiberglass for the bodywork and subsequent use of magnesium, aluminum, carbon fiber, and even balsa wood in the design of its suspension, to the far-rear placement of its transmission to keep the Corvette light, responsive, and balanced, and to expand its dynamic capabilities with each new generation.

While those common denominators also marked the development and design of the seventh-generation sports car, Juechter pointed to another factor that enabled and empowered the new Corvette's creation. "We got the band back together," he said.

The band—Tom Peters, Kirk Bennion, Harlan Charles, and Tadge Juechter—comprise a quartet that brings together mutual history with the Corvette as well as respect for each other. "We respect each other enough that we know good ideas can come from anywhere," Juechter said.

Though Tom Peters and Kirk Bennion work in design, Harlan Charles in product planning (marketing), and Juechter as an engineer, "we can swim outside our lanes," Juechter said, adding that while each cares about his own area of specific expertise and responsibility, they all care more about the car itself and the expectations and needs of its future owners.

Not only do the band members like and respect each other, they are liked and respected by the Corvette community, many of whom they know on a first-name basis from their regular attendance at weekend Corvette gatherings across the country. Just as the car becomes a lifestyle for its customers, so too is creating and improving the car more than a vocation—it's an avocation for the design, engineering, and marketing teams.

Sure, there are disagreements along the way, but Juechter said that Ed Welburn, GM's vice president of design, has been open about the fact that probably for the first time in the history of the Corvette—with the possible exception of the original Motorama car—the seventh-generation sports car was the first created without heated battles between engineering and design. In fact, the development of the C7 is being used within GM as an example of how design, engineering, marketing, and production can work together for the greater good.

BUT IS IT FAST?

Of course, chief among Corvette community events are racecars doing what they do best: racing.

As early as 1954, Corvettes, with their six-cylinder engines, were racing against Jaguars and other imports in Sports Car Club of America events and even facing off in the famed Mexican road race. Things accelerated—quite literally—when Chevrolet began installing its small-block V-8 engine in the car. There were speed runs on Daytona Beach, racing in the 12-hour event at Sebring—including a class victory and ninth-overall finish by Corvette drivers John Fitch and Walt Hansgen in 1956—and a class victory in 1960 in the famed 24 Hours of Le Mans race, with Fitch and Bob Grossman finishing eighth overall behind six Ferraris and an Aston Martin.

Zora Arkus-Duntov and even design director Bill Mitchell played important roles in Corvette racing. Later, Herb Fishel took charge of General Motors' motorsports efforts and, when it came to road racing, worked closely with Michigan-based racing car builder Pratt & Miller and its racing team manager, Doug Fehan. Fehan guided championship efforts ranging from a Chevrolet sedan-based Trans-Am title to an IMSA crown won with an Oldsmobile Aurora V-8–powered, mid-engine Le Mans-style prototype.

In 1996, with the fifth-generation Corvette in development, Fehan laid out a plan for Chevrolet management that he was confident would pay dividends down the road—"Although it was a dramatic change from the way we had been doing business, I actually felt we had a very good chance of it being accepted."

"A lot of manufacturers talk about racing technology and filtering it back into their production cars," Fehan said as he recalled the meeting. "But there was no place in the industry where it has developed as strongly as what I thought we could do with the Corvette." Dave Hill, then chief engineer for Corvette, was strongly on board, as was Fishel.

"The presentation I made was about thirty-five or forty minutes long," Fehan said. That presentation basically asked Chevrolet to back a program that would consume two years getting the C5 ready to race. There would be no racing, just a lot of expense getting ready to race the right way. And what was the right way?

In 2010, Corvette Racing celebrated the 50th anniversary of the car in competition at Le Mans with a special event at the Laguna Seca track in northern California, where the cars included the No. 2 car from 1960, the No. 49 car from 1969, the No. 9 car from 1967, the No. 4 C6R GT2 from the 2010 racing season, and the first 2011 GM Design Special Anniversary Corvette Z06.

Racing, winning, and racing and winning with technology that could transfer from the track to the street and even from the street to the track. "A program that truly respected the technologies Chevrolet had in-house," was how Fehan put it. "I knew this made sense," he added. "I'd done this all my life."

But, he also knew, there was significant risk in asking any company to put its money—in "not insignificant numbers"—behind Fehan's bold plan.

"At the end of the presentation, people's body language made it look like they thought it was nuts," Fehan realized. But then John Middlebrook, the general manager of the Chevrolet division, "took his glasses off and rubbed his eyes and said, 'Doug, I'm a GM lifer, and this is the first racing program I've seen that really made sense.'"

After Middlebrook's endorsement, the round-the-table vote was a mere formality. Pratt & Miller began development, keeping in close communication with the Corvette engineering team led by Hill (and later by Tom Wallace and then by Tadge Juechter), of what would launch in 1999 as the C5-R—Corvette generation-5 Racer—and, with the introduction of the C6 Corvette, the C6-R.

BEYOND THE CHECKERED FLAG

After a shakedown season at the races in 1999, "Duntov's dream of a full factory-backed Corvette racing program was about to be realized," David Kimble writes in his history of Corvette racing. And the result?

Eight consecutive American Le Mans Series GT1 championships from 2001 through 2008.

But perhaps just as important was the effect the racing team had on the production Corvettes—especially the C7. After winning at Le Mans in 2001 and 2002, the team came in second to Ferrari in 2003. The team thought it knew the reason—tires. Ferrari's tires were better than the Corvette's.

But simply switching tires was no easy matter. Corvette (indeed, all of General Motors) had a long corporate relationship with Goodyear, which supplied the tires on Corvettes for the road and the track. But racers being racers, with their *gotta-win* determination, the team returned to the United States from Le Mans, obtained a set of Michelins on the sly, rented a racetrack in secret, mounted the Michelins on one of its racecars, and was astounded once the checkered flag was waved.

The car wasn't just a few tenths of a second faster. It was several seconds faster. Per lap.

With real data to show the difference, the racing team went to GM, received permission to switch brands for 2004, and won—and won again, and won again—at Le Mans and elsewhere.

"Michelin and GM did not have a very good working relationship at that point, so we had mountains to climb," Fehan said. However, he added, "the Michelin experience was not wasted on Chevrolet or GM." Beginning in 2008, Michelin offered an aftermarket tire especially engineered for Corvettes (improving wet and dry grip and shortening stopping distances) and since then has offered aftermarket tires to several of GM's best performance vehicles, including the Z06 and ZR1 versions of the C6. They would all have the ability to ride on original-equipment Michelins, as will all seventh-generation Corvettes.

Underscoring the technology transfer from the track to the road is the fact that the same engineers who developed the Michelin tires for the Corvette racing team developed the Michelin tires for the 2014 Stingray.

In developing the C7, Juechter said, the strategy was "how does the racecar work better, and can we apply any of those strategies to the street?"

Several aspects of the racing car not only improved the seventh-generation production Corvette, but also influenced its new dynamic design. Or, as Juechter put it, "things taken straight off the racecar but 'done pretty' for the street."

The developments are exciting. On the racetrack, air used to cool the engine is vented through a vent cut into the car's hood. That air then passes over the car's roof instead of beneath the car, enhancing downforce. "Taking air over the car instead of under is a tremendous benefit for lift," Juechter said, adding that in the production version, as much as 40 percent of the airflow is directed over the roof.

The C6R competes at Le Mans in the 2011 edition of the famed 24-hour race.

"It's a big paradigm shift for front lift," he added, explaining that the typical way to increase front-end downforce is to bolt "huge splitters," a lower valance, beneath the front bumper. That works—at least until you hit a curb or speed bump. It's much better, he said, to be able to reduce lift with the fundamental shape of the car.

"We are partners with our racing team," the chief engineer said. "Most companies say they are racing-inspired, which means nothing. Ours is racing reality. . . I have no embarrassment saying we started with the racing team's solutions."

Another example involves cooling the Stingray's differential and transmission, both of which are mounted at the back of the chassis. Traditionally, such units are cooled by radiators mounted at the front of the car, where they can benefit from the airflow. But that means having to snake all sorts of ducting back to reach the components that need to be cooled.

The racing team simply cuts NACA ducts into the rear quarter panels of the C6-R to draw in that cooling air. For the Stingray, engineers and designers came up with an effective but much more elegantly aesthetic solution. Not only did they

Hot on the tail of the C6R will be the C7R, poised to make its competitive debut in the 24 Hours of Daytona race early in 2014.

follow the racing team's lead by moving those radiators to the rear, they supply cooling air through specially designed vents atop the quarter panels and then exhaust that air through virtually hidden venting not only in the lower rear fascia, but also around the tail lamps.

Fehan noted that the racing team also contributes to the production development team's knowledge and understanding of high-speed aerodynamics. "You can't do 200 miles per hour in the GM wind tunnel," he said. "Tadge wasn't reluctant [to take advantage of the racing effort]. He saw the resource that was there. It became abundantly clear to him that the more he learned from racing, the better product he was going to get for his customers."

Fehan also pointed to one other benefit the racing team brings to the Corvette, though this time to the marketing effort: "In every country but the United States, Le Mans is a huge deal. Six hundred and fifty million people watch on television, and 350,000 are in attendance at the race. National Geographic declared it the best sporting event in the world in 2011. By virtue of what we have accomplished there, we have put Corvette and Chevrolet on the [global car-buying] map and garnered global respect for what Chevrolet and General Motors can accomplish: the durability and reliability of the cars."

At the same time, improving the production car also helps the racing team, which competes in classes based on production vehicles. The C7R is scheduled to make its debut in the 24 Hours of Daytona race early in 2014.

Fehan notes that while the racing team helped make the road car better, changes made by the engineering and design teams will help provide an even better basis for the racer.

"I call it cascade engineering," he said, explaining that racing helps the road car and the road car helps racing and then racing helps with the next road car and that next road car helps the racing team.

"In the past, Corvette has been uniquely American in so many ways, and there's nothing wrong with that," Fehan said. "But the sophistication and edginess they have put into this new design is expanding its reach. It's a global design, but also so is Corvette. This is going to reach people far more broadly than in the past. The world is looking for the C7."

Doug Fehan was instrumental in incorporating racing technology into the C6 and C7.

CHAPTER

3 EXTERIOR

Kirk Bennion remembers during the depths of the financial doldrums that eventually would force General Motors through a government-mandated bankruptcy, the GM Design team resolved to re-envision many of the cars they knew so well, prompting some of the best conceptual work during some of GM's darkest hours.

Typically, Bennion and his fellow designers, sculptors, engineers, and others who work within the GM design studios at the campus-style GM Tech Center facilities in Warren, Michigan, are busy with more than 60 programs in various stages of execution, from early concepts to facelifts of vehicles already in production. But with financial resources in increasingly short supply—indeed, with the company bleeding money and its survival as a viable automaker in jeopardy—there came a point when the team was forced to set some projects aside and focus on an uncertain future.

To make the best use of the downtime and to keep spirits within the studios as elevated as possible, the designers let their minds wander, dreaming up a few *what if?* scenarios. One idea compelled them more than the rest: What if there really is a next-generation Corvette? What should it be? What could it be?

Not long out of design school, Bennion had been part of the team in the middle and late 1980s that contributed early concepts for what was expected to become the next Chevrolet Corvette, the fifth-generation (C5) version of America's sports car. That new car's production launch was anticipated in the early 1990s, but because of another cycle of economic woes, it wasn't until 1997 that the fifth-generation Corvette actually rolled off the assembly line. By then, Bennion was busy designing trucks.

DESIGN

The Stingray concept car was the basis for the *Transformers* movie character named Sideswipe.

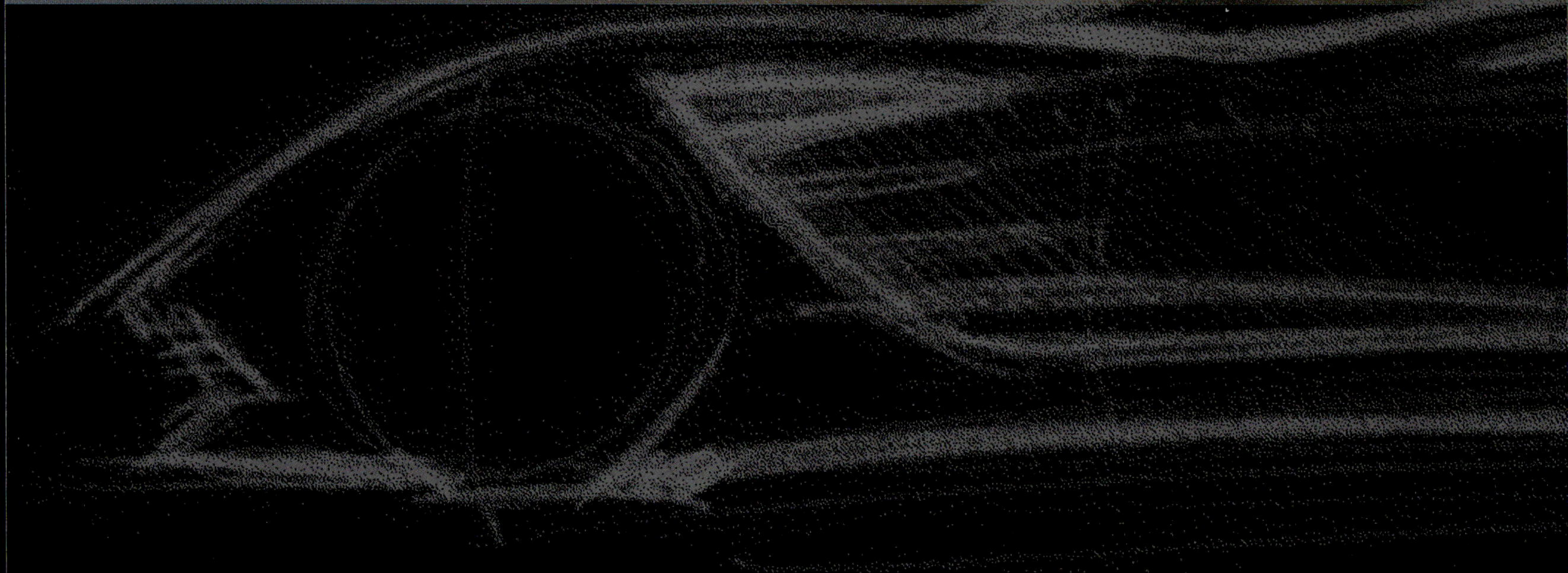

Nonetheless, Bennion knew that "it was a good time to get acquainted with the car and for a squeaky kid out of college to get the tribal knowledge" about such an automotive icon.

That early experience with the Corvette proved especially good when Bennion returned to the sports car studio—he served as lead exterior designer for the sixth-generation Corvette that made its debut as a 2005 model.

It was the successor to that car on which he and the others in the studio started work in 2007. Started, that is, but soon halted. The program, Bennion said, "ended up getting canceled."

But if a seventh-generation Corvette was on hold, perhaps, the designers hoped, there still would be a C6.5, "a minor facelift with some architectural stuff," as Bennion put it.

"But that ended up getting canceled, too," he said. "The checkbook was dry."

In fact, the checkbook was so dry that the federal government stepped in to save not just General Motors, but the entire American domestic auto industry, including its suppliers. To survive, GM had to cancel not just individual car programs but entire automotive divisions. Pontiac is no more.

General Motors emerged from bankruptcy with just four automotive brands for North America—Chevrolet, Cadillac, Buick, and GMC. Chevrolet, the largest and mainstream brand, and Cadillac, the luxury marque, would expand their distribution to markets around the world. Buick was already hugely popular in China, and growing steadily in North America. GMC was an historic truck brand that would provide a way for Cadillac and Buick dealers to profit by selling modified versions of Chevrolet's pickup trucks, sport, and crossover utility vehicles.

And, to the surprise of many people, part of this new GM product portfolio would be a new Corvette.

When representatives of the U.S. Treasury Department and the president's automotive task force began examining General Motors and its finances, they discovered some surprising things about the Corvette. Despite its relatively low sales volumes, and in an era of flexible production—multiple models being built on the same assembly line—this car was constructed in a dedicated assembly plant. What's more, the Corvette was a profitable vehicle for the company, and it didn't hurt that at least some of the federal examiners were car enthusiasts who couldn't bear the thought of putting an end to the sports car's production.

So, very, very quietly, under orders of absolute secrecy, Ed Welburn (GM's global vice president for design) invited not just the designers in Warren, but also those in every GM design studio around the globe, to submit sketches for what they thought the next-generation Chevrolet Corvette should be.

This "global sketch blitz" was a first for the design of a Corvette, for which all styling had previously been done within the corporation's U.S. studios. But by seeking input from around the GM world, Welburn not only exposed GM to new ideas, but also created a fresh enthusiasm within the GM Design community.

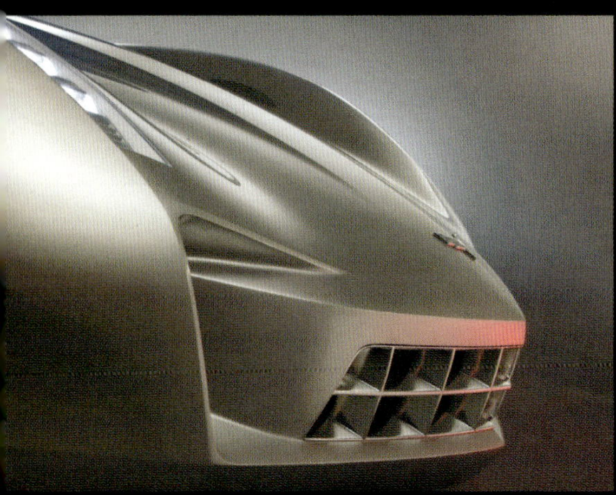

General Motors designers from studios around the world were invited to submit sketches showing their ideas for a seventh-generation Chevrolet Corvette. Here are some of the 300 or more that were submitted.

"It was a great perk for people to get to sketch on the car who otherwise never would get to," said Bennion, whose job it was to collect those sketches and to begin their review. "We probably got over three hundred sketches," he reported.

Not only was the volume encouraging, but so were the sketches themselves. Ryan Vaughan was the designer who would help lead the team doing the new Corvette's interior, and as he explained it, even people who worked in overseas design studios and who had never seen a Corvette in person demonstrated with their sketches that they understood the car, its essence, and its mission. As Vaughan put it, everyone was "all orbiting around the same idea."

FROM PAPER TO PAVEMENT

Part of establishing the early vision for the next-generation Corvette—should there actually be one—involved the design and development of a Corvette-based car for the second installment in Michael Bay's *Transformers* movies.

In the summer of 2007, the resurrected Chevrolet Camaro was introduced as a character in a Steven Spielberg/Michael Bay box-office-hit movie based on the popular Transformers comic books and toys. For the movie's 2009 sequel, the script included a Corvette-based character named Sideswipe. At the Chicago auto show in February of that same year, just a few months before the movie's premiere, GM unveiled a swoopy, low-slung Corvette concept car, the car on which Sideswipe was based. Perhaps more significant, however, was the concept car's name—Stingray.

The Stingray/Sideswipe concept and character grew out of a scale model that had been sitting in General Motors' Advanced Design Studio in Michigan even before the first Transformers movie was shot. The movie's director, Michael Bay, had toured the studio and noticed the model—it was a modern interpretation of the classic 1963 split-window Corvette coupe. He had wondered if he might use it as the basis for a character in what he knew would be a series of Transformers movies.

GM designers were delighted in part because they wanted to see just how far they could push the "Corvette statement" and still have a car the public would recognize as a Corvette, but also in part because they wanted to see if they could translate the essence of the historic Stingrays in contemporary, even futuristic ways.

They also were eager to revive the historic Stingray name, and not merely as a concept car but perhaps even applying it to a 6.5 version of the Corvette itself, said Tom Peters, director of exterior design for GM performance cars and full-size trucks and a veteran of both the Corvette and Camaro studios.

But their boss, GM Global Design chief Ed Welburn, wasn't sure about reviving the Stingray badge just yet.

"Ed said we have to wait until there's a car that really lives up to that, to the Stingray name. He would not support a C6 Stingray facelift," Peters said, "and that was the right thing to do."

The Stingray concept displayed at Chicago was inspiring, though the eventual approved Stingray chassis and design were not lifted from the concept car of the same name. Peters and Welburn agreed, however, that the design—its philosophy and form vocabulary—were intriguing, so a slightly smaller (7⁄8-scale) version was developed and became the running concept shown at Chicago.

"Before the [C7] program even began, we had the Stingray concept and there were those in the company who asked if this is the next-generation Corvette," Welburn picked up the story. "I said no," Welburn responded. "It was a great styling exercise, a concept with a role in the movie and we could develop that into the the C7, but I said I wanted to beat that design."

As for the Stingray badge on the C7, Welburn admitted to being stubborn.

"Whenever I'm asked what my absolute favorite car is, to those who really don't know everything about Corvettes, I say it's the '63 Sting Ray coupe," Welburn said. "And to those who really know Corvettes, I tell them it's the '59 Stingray racer."

Welburn said both his favorites are amazing cars. "There is just a whole emotion, a form vocabulary, a muscle tension in those designs and it is really, really special.

"There have been a lot of great Corvettes," he continued. "I own a C4 and love it. But I would never call it a Stingray.

"There is not a checklist that makes a car at Stingray," he added. Instead, he said, "it's an emotion, a feeling, a form vocabulary. As this car developed, I saw the emerge, a muscle tension, a sophistication in the design that made it a Stingray."

Welburn also explained the confusion over the spelling of the word "Stingray" —or is it "StingRay" or "Sting Ray" or, as on signage at the car's unveiling, STINGRAY, in all capital letters, but with the S and the R as slightly larger letters but positioned to extend slightly below the baseline.

"It's one word," Welburn said, "Not with a captial R but," he teased, "there is a bit of an emphasis on the R."

Peters had a long history with the Corvette. He was responsible for several historic Corvette concept vehicles and, as the head of the performance vehicle studio, his new responsibilities included overseeing the development of styling for any new Corvette, with Bennion managing the exterior design process on a day-to-day basis.

"Kirk and I have been involved with Corvette for many, many years," Peters said. "There's a lot of history and experience, and both of us are in this business because we have great passion for cars like this. Everybody remembers their first ride in a Corvette. It's special. There is a certain magic about Corvette. It's more than a product. When you design cars like this, you're creating an individual with personality. When cars are done right, people relate to them on an emotional level."

For the seventh generation, that personality had to remain fully American, but at the same time speak more strongly to potential buyers in other countries, where the car was becoming increasingly popular because of its success in international sports car races, including the 24 Hours of Le Mans. In the United States, there are so many Corvette enthusiasts that sales of any new version seem almost automatic. But to sell overseas, the new car would have to compete against the world's best and most exotic sports cars from Italy, Germany, Japan, and England. "It needed to be different, more expressive, appealing on a global level," Bennion said. "We needed to raise the level of sophistication while keeping all of that raw power."

A EUROPEAN RACER IN AMERICA

In 1959, Bill Mitchell succeeded Harley Earl as head of General Motors design. It was Earl who had created the original Corvette, an open sports car designed to give Americans an alternative to the deft (if low-powered) roadsters that many American servicemen brought home from Europe after World War II. Mitchell was responsible for transforming that car's design from merely cute into something that would live up to the newfound performance potential provided when racer-turned-GM engineer Zora Arkus-Duntov put a V-8 engine beneath the Corvette's fiberglass hood, a manual transmission between the seats, and serious suspension beneath the car itself. Earl and Mitchell were determined to make an American driving and racing machine unlike any other seen before it. And with Arkus-Duntov's help, they had a good chance to do it.

Arkus-Duntov was a racer. He had driven in the 24 Hours of Le Mans and other sports car races in Europe. But while Mitchell might not have been as accomplished as a driver, he was a dedicated racing enthusiast who had grown up with the Collier brothers, Miles and Sam, who in the 1930s started a racing club that evolved into the Sports Car Club of America.

As the new GM styling vice-president, Mitchell was in a position to pursue his passions. He assigned young GM designer, Larry Shinoda, create special bodywork for a Corvette-based racing car that Mitchell would enter in SCCA events. In honor of its smooth, aerodynamic styling and Mitchell's affection for saltwater sport fishing, there was only one name for the dynamic new vehicle—the Stingray.

Mitchell turned the car over to driver Dr. Dick Thompson, who steered the Stingray to the SCCA national championship in the C-Modified class. After a season of racing, the car went on the auto show circuit, and then Mitchell used the Stingray as his daily driver for his commute from home to the studios.

In those studios, Mitchell assigned Shinoda and others to work on the car that would launch the Corvette brand into its second generation and toward its high-performance potential. Because of its unique rear-window design, that car would forever be known and cherished by car collectors as the "split-window" Corvette. That 1963 model was also the first Corvette to roll off the assembly line with an

additional badge on its flanks. *Sting Ray*, the badge read.

Arkus-Duntov was especially proud. "For the first time," he proclaimed at the car's launch, "I now have a Corvette I can be proud to drive in Europe."

Although the split-window feature was a one-year wonder, the Sting Ray (or Stingray) name would be used on various second-generation Corvette models and on Corvette dream-machine concept cars in 1992 and 2009.

"Stingray is one of the hallowed names in automotive history," Welburn said. "We knew we couldn't use the Stingray name unless the new car truly lived up to the legacy."

Those early vision design meetings and ongoing discussions with Corvette engineers established some of the elements that forever changed the way the seventh-generation Corvette looked. For example, the car's track and wheelbase would be lengthened, the engine would be moved slightly to the rear, and there would need to be a way to supply cooling airflow to powertrain components whether they were mounted beneath the hood or at the very rear of the car. Nonetheless, this revised vision still left plenty of room for specific interpretation, and the studio began culling the hundreds of designs from around the world.

"We identified a few key goals," Bennion said of the C7 mission statement for design: "a new form vocabulary, a new surface we hadn't seen before on the Corvette—bolder, more assertive—a more serious front end, new upper, and the lamp graphics needed to push the envelope." Lighting needed to be not only state-of-the-art but also presented "in a new aesthetic package."

Oh, and in addition to all of that, the car still had to be immediately recognizable as a Corvette. Whether viewed in static display at an auto show or glimpsed as it rocketed down the highway or racetrack, the Corvette needed to be as visible and recognizable as it always was. But how, Bennion was asked, does the team go through the process of paring down 300 drawings to something more manageable?

"It was like walking through a parking lot and suddenly one car jumps out to you," he responded.

The designs that jumped out seemed to resonate with both the engineering and aesthetic goals for the car, and the designers were allowed to develop their ideas through a series of two-dimensional drawings. Those whose drawings showed further promise were invited to produce three-dimensional scale models.

Bennion and other design leaders saw "a lot" of scale models in 2009, he said, with detail and definition improving as the models evolved. In 2010, the studio was in a position to look at the best of the best of them in the form of full-scale clay models.

Among those submitting sketches for the Corvette global design blitz was Hwasup Lee, who was born in South Korea but moved to the United States while in high school. He studied at the famed Art Center College of Design in southern California and was hired by GM after his graduation. As his early sketches show, he drew inspiration from the past as he looked toward Corvette's future. The inset image (top right) shows one of the Corvette SS racers from the mid-1950s.

Throughout the process, there were monthly design reviews with Welburn and Mark Reuss, a long-time GM engineer (as well as a licensed racing driver) who started the GM Performance Division, later ran the company's Australian arm (Holden), and was GM's overall vice president of engineering before becoming president of GM's North American operations in 2009. Bennion said Reuss and Welburn were really "into" the Corvette program. "They had both feet in the pool," is how he put it.

So did GM's new chief executive, Dan Akerson, who toured GM Design with Welburn in the fall of 2010 and asked in particular about the status of a new Corvette, expressing his enthusiasm and praise for the project.

The program received another energizing endorsement in January, 2011, when a program review was held in the GM Heritage Center, the company's private collection of important and historic vehicles. At the review, the C7 was parked under a cover among both Corvette production and concept vehicles. When the cover was removed, there was spontaneous applause and a standing ovation.

In the Corvette's 60-year history, this car would be only the seventh all-new model. For Welburn, it would be the first created under his tenure as head of GM Design.

Among the sketches that jumped out at Peters early on were those by Hwasup Lee, a young designer who was born in South Korea. Lee moved to the United States while in junior high school and joined GM in 2000 after studying at the Art Center College of Design in Pasadena, California. Almost immediately, he was responsible for designing a concept that would be unveiled as the 2001 GMC TerraCross. He worked in the GM truck studio and then went into advanced design, first in the United States and then in England. In 2005 he produced another GMC concept, worked on some preproduction programs for Cadillac, and was lead exterior designer for a global small crossover utility vehicle being sold in North America as the Buick Encore and Chevrolet Trax.

In 2008, his work on those vehicles completed, he was invited into Tom Peters' Performance Vehicle studio, where he was lead exterior designer for the ZL1 version of the Chevrolet Camaro. He also submitted his ideas for the new Corvette.

"The challenge," Lee said of his early Corvette proposals, "was to create a new and fresh statement while making sure that anyone would be able to recognize it as a Corvette." To achieve that goal, he looked to fresh sources of inspiration, as well as into the "great history" of the Corvette.

Lee wanted to pack as much emotion and intrigue into his design as its history warranted, but at the same time to needed to show its structural balance and even some sort of unnameable sophistication. His inspiration included the latest in jet-fighter aircraft, but also elements he saw in the work of contemporary architects.

Tom Peters, head of GM's Performance Vehicle design studio, and Kirk Bennion, lead designer for the C7 Corvette, liked Hwasup Lee's ideas and gave him time to evolve them into a more mature yet still aggressive theme.

This illustration shows Hwasup Lee's final theme proposal for the C7 Corvette.

For historical reference, he focused on vehicles such as the 1957 Corvette SS (an Arkus-Duntov Corvette racing car), and the 1969 Manta Ray, another Corvette concept car.

To instill emotion in the car's design, Lee sketched and then developed what he called "strong interactions" between the car's various surfaces and "hard-edge dynamics" that encourage the viewer's eyes not only to see the car as a whole, but also to examine every surface and interface as they move over the car.

Lee's design included a lot of curvature in its sections and also how those curves accelerated into what he called "very crisp" edges. The result, he said, was a tension and muscularity that displayed both speed and gracefulness, producing a fresh, new, and distinct design theme that was still uniquely Corvette.

But Lee's wasn't the only theme being developed. Welburn had set up an internal competition.

"Management identified two themes and asked us to develop them to full size," Bennion said, saying that Lee's car emphasized the Corvette's front-mid engine placement and almost mid-engine architectural profile, while the other model featured longer front fenders and a more subordinated rear section.

"If you're a swimmer," Peters explained, "and you're shooting for a really good time, you swim as hard as you can, but you'll never get as fast as when you have a buddy racing against you. The car's sophistication and design quality rose through this competition.

"We had two really strong designs," Peters said, adding that Lee's design won in dramatic fashion, like an Olympic swimmer coming from behind to win the race.

This illustration shows where Hwasup Lee had taken his theme in the early summer of 2010.

This illustration shows a similar vantage, though was done more than a year later and is much closer in detail to the car that would be unveiled at the North American International Auto Show early in 2013.

"Ed was not convinced at first with this [Lee's] direction," said Peters, who had worked with Lee in the performance studio and knew the young designer's skill and potential.

In its early state, Lee's design needed more finesse, but it had a strong spirit, and Peters asked Welburn to let the studio team sort some things out.

"He didn't say no," Peters said. "He was confident enough in us to let us pursue it longer and the guys did a wonderful job to refine the design."

And that redefined theme would set the direction for the new seventh-generation Corvette.

"After the selection was made, the whole design team came together and continued the development," Peters said, adding that while one design wins out, "we continued to draw from one another to incorporate the best details into the finished car.

"Tom Peters is one of the most visionary designers I know," Ed Welburn said. "He sees things others don't. I wanted to give him the space and the time to develop those ideas. Over time, I've learned that the best results come from Tom when I give him space and time. It's all about providing an environment in which people feel free to create and to explore and to try new things.

"I have to be patient," Welburn added, "but great things happen."

Even after that winning theme was determined, Bennion said, it still had to be developed with the final combination of details fitting together, producing not only an aesthetically pleasing vehicle, but one that is purely Corvette. First, he said, the body side was "nailed down," and then the front of the car was detailed, and finally the back section of the car was blended in to produce a "complete envelope." And though the decision to go with the Lee design was made in the summer of 2010, the work was far from finished.

"We pulled the strengths from each of the cars, developed the back end a little further, a little tighter, and adjusted surfaces for lower coefficient of drag while still keeping them aesthetically pleasing," Bennion said.

Overall, he added, the car was tightened and overhangs shortened, with fine-tuning both from the skilled hands of the GM design sculptors, working both digitally and hands-on in clay, and in the numbers generated as the full-scale car was evaluated in the GM wind tunnel.

"The car has very sculptural intersections," Bennion explained. "There's nothing too straightforward or simple. There's an interest to it," he said, pointing to the overlapping between the front fenders and the hood, and then between the hood and its air extractor. "These are unique, compelling, and intriguing surface developments," he said, and yet they were consistent with the mandate that on the Stingray, all forms have a genuine function.

At the same time, however, care must be taken not to overwork a surface to the point of stripping it of its emotional impact, its personality. "You can overwork the surface and take some of the personality from it," Bennion said. "It's a matter of finesse."

Jelani Aliyu from GM Design checks the surface detailing of a full-scale clay model of the new Corvette Stingray.

The Stingray's exterior design shows much finesse from front to rear, for example, from the way the hood duct not only helps cool the engine, but also produces airflow that increases front-end downforce to the way that air taken into cooled rear powertrain components exits not only from the lower section of the rear fascia, but also through ducting around the tail lamps. Such solutions are clever and also done in such a way as to be functional while enhancing the visual aesthetic. Call it the synergy of form and function.

Bennion also pointed out how the car's side cove continues a Corvette tradition but leans a little more forward, lending more speed to the car's profile.

On the other hand, gone from the side view is the old "basket handle" roofline, which in the coupe has been replaced by a more fastback profile with a fixed rear quarter window and an aesthetic gesture that emphasizes the muscular rear fenders and the power the rear wheels put to the pavement.

Two-dimensional design sketches only take the design process so far. Eventually, three dimensions are needed and take shape first as scale-model clay sculptures and later as full-size models. To maximize the process, those models often show different designs on their left and right sides, with mirrors positioned to trick the eye so it thinks it's seeing a complete vehicle.

The car's rear view has changed as well. The traditional Corvette elements and the relationship between the dual paired tail lamps and license plate position remain, but now they're designed to give the car's tail a more "exotic car" appearance.

Even the crossed-flag Corvette emblem was redesigned to show more gesture, more speed. Even its placement was evaluated to enhance both appearance and aerodynamics, emblems are inset into the bodywork as part of a detailed design and engineering effort that looked at "every millimeter" of the car.

From the start, the new Corvette was designed as an open car, whether as a coupe featuring a removable panel over the seats or as a full convertible with a canvas-material top that folds away beneath an integrated tonneau cover to expose the entire passenger compartment (not to mention the Corvette convertible's trademark body-colored waterfall between the seats) to the car's surroundings.

"It's not just a styling statement. It's a very serious machine capable of speeds of around 200 miles per hour. It's a weapon, and every millimeter is taken into consideration," Peters said. But Bennion finished the sentence, "nothing has been compromised. There's nothing we have to talk around. There's more sculpture. More section. And it all adds to the aesthetic. It's not just putting a scoop here or there. It's beautifully integrated."

And, for its seventh generation, the Corvette is just as beautiful on the inside as on the outside.

The Stingray Design team considers a couple of full-size scale models in the private courtyard at the GM Tech Center. Note how the mirror is positioned so viewers can see the full rear end of the vehicle, even though the clay model holds two different design proposals.

Tom Peters checks a hood detail as he prepares the full-scale model for evaluation.

These are full-scale clay models covered with silver decal film so they look like finished vehicles. C7 proposals are displayed side by side for evaluation.

Ed Welburn and other studio leaders take a more distant perspective as they consider the theme and details of a full-scale model for the C7.

Skilled sculptors work closely with designers to shape the specific contours and details of the seventh-generation Chevrolet Corvette into clay. Once the clay model is completed, computer measuring devices are used to create a mathematical model that can be used for fabricating body panels for production.

CHAPTER

4 INTERIOR

When the supercar combined its V-8 engine, its aerodynamic shape, and amazing technology (including a suspension system that literally and figuratively used magnets to stick it to the road), the Chevrolet Corvette became not just a world-class sports car, but one that provided a bang for the buck unmatched by any other even relatively mass-marketed sports car available.

There was one aspect of the Corvette, though, that fell short of its higher-priced competition: the interior compartment occupied by the driver and passenger.

It wasn't that the Corvette's twin-cockpit design wasn't practical—features such as a heads-up display are terrific whether you're on the highway or the racetrack. It was just that the materials, the finishes, and the detailing were—how should I put this?—not the most luxurious. Critics and potential customers saw the car as, well, incomplete.

"The interior gets hammered," admitted Tom Peters, who oversees the design of Chevrolet's highest-performance vehicles. "We felt we made a great step from the C5 to the C6," he said. But, he acknowledged, while there had been more emphasis on the design of the interior for the C6, the business case allowed only so much to be invested in materials and finishes.

Just about the time the C6 rolled off the assembly line (and thus too late for the sixth-gen Corvette), General Motors made a commitment to upgrading—significantly upgrading—the interiors of all of its new vehicles.

Including, of course, any future Corvettes.

CORVETTE

DESIGN

As with the exterior for the new Stingray, GM Design staged a global interior sketch blitz to draw ideas from all of the company's designers in studios around the world. Here are some of the entries.

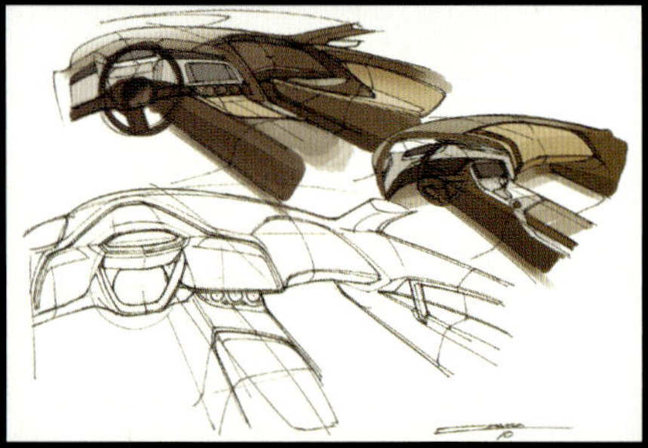

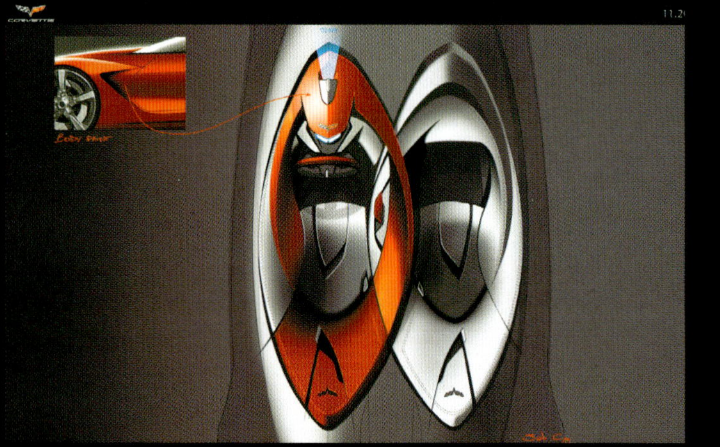

As with the exterior for the new Stingray, GM Design staged a global interior sketch blitz to draw ideas from all of the company's designers in studios around the world. Here are some of the entries.

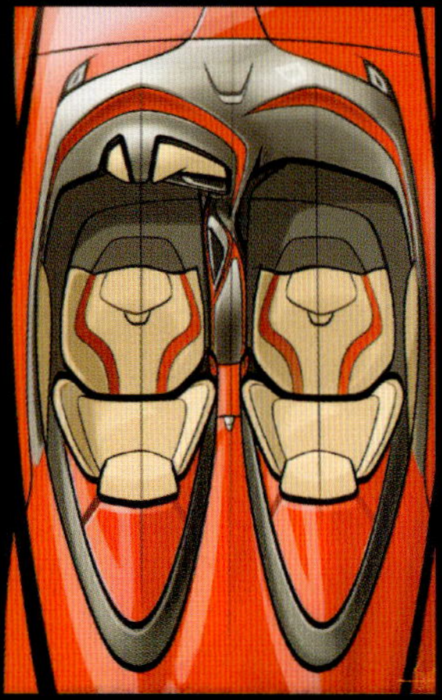

So, in the summer of 2009, designers in all General Motors styling studios were invited to participate in a global sketch blitz, submitting their ideas for what the interior of a new Corvette could and should be. Submitted designs were collected and collated, and some were selected for further refinement.

Three primary themes were identified and further refined. Just before the end-of-the-year holiday break, three prospective interior designs were refined and submitted to Ed Welburn, GM's global vice president of design, who would select which would go into the next-generation Corvette.

Welburn made his decision. It was a decision that demonstrated, perhaps more than any of the vehicles designed during his reign, the strength of his leadership. Welburn decided that none of the three finalists was good enough.

"We came back from break, and he said, 'start over,'" Ryan Vaughan remembered.

"He was right," Vaughan confirms. "Those three themes did not go far enough in pushing this thing forward and transforming it."

While Vaughan might have recognized the wisdom in Welburn's decision, he also knew the decision brought a new dimension into the work of whoever would be chosen to design the interior for the seventh-generation Corvette. "Their hair's on fire at that point," said Vaughan.

As it turned out, it would be Vaughan whose hair would be ignited.

"I didn't ask them to start over," Welburn responded. "They learned a lot from that initial design blitz." Welburn said there actually were four themes that were "good." But, he added, "they weren't great."

"Corvette interiors have not been strong since the '63 Sting Ray, which had a great interior," Welburn continued. "The next generation car had a phenominal interior as well, but they have not been significant since then, though the C6 was good. But it was time for something very significant. I wanted them to dig down deep."

Welburn praised Helen Emsley, director of the performance-car interior design studio, for organizing "a real design competition."

"We spent a lot of time sifting through those designs with her," Welburn said. "I get really close up to the design process, roll my sleeves up and work with the team. It's a very intimate thing, and through that process, something very special emerged. The design that emerged was something the whole design organization could stand behind, rally behind, and everyone did everything they could to make it happen."

"We could have developed one of those first-gen [initial sketch blitz] themes, but when they dug down, they developed something that was strong."

EMOTIONAL, DRAMATIC, AND FUNCTIONAL

Ryan Vaughan had been working at GM Design for eight years (longer if you include his internship there while studying industrial design at New York's famed Pratt Institute). After graduation, Vaughan joined GM Design full-time as an interior designer. Almost immediately, he saw sketches developed into the interior for the Pontiac G6 concept car unveiled at the North American International Auto Show in Detroit in January 2003.

Vaughan worked on the interiors for the Saturn Aura, Chevrolet Malibu, and Buick LaCrosse as well, finishing his work on the LaCrosse while working out of the GM design studio in China, where the Buick brand is extremely popular. He also worked in the GM studio in Brazil, where he created interiors for GM vehicles designed for drivers in emerging markets. He returned to GM Design in Michigan just as Welburn was launching a second sketch blitz for the Corvette interior.

Again, the entries were gathered and judged. Again, some were selected for further development, and finally—again—there were three finalists. Vaughan was surprised to learn that he was one of them and that his vision was selected to progress—perhaps even into production.

Each of the three final sketch themes garnered support within GM Design. They were shared with a focus group of sports car owners in southern California—some Corvette owners were included, but most had opted to buy other brands, especially German brands. Vaughan's theme "popped out as being the preferred design," he recalled, and was transformed from two to three dimensions in clay back in Michigan. But, Vaughan knew, "it was still up for grabs," pending one final review with Welburn.

"It was just before Easter 2010," Vaughan said. "Ed saw the raw clay and said 'that's it.'"

"We had exceptional freedom," Vaughan said of the charge given to what would become his C7 interior design team. "Everybody recognized the need to truly transform the interior. Ergonomically, the current [C6] interior is very good. The materials get a bum rap, because it has fairly good materials. But we knew we could upgrade that and the technology and the design. The current [C6] design is sober and functional. We wanted something more emotional, but not distracting. Something more dramatic."

Emotional, dramatic, functional—something every competitive (and casual) driver desires.

"The Corvette is such a serious car, so it has to be super functional," Vaughan knew.

"We had our challenges on the exterior," added Kirk Bennion, exterior design manager for the Corvette Stingray. "But the interior, those guys had to come even further," Bennion says. "They had to make the most improvement on the car. Everything they did had the challenge to make the biggest leap, an interior Renaissance." Vaughan recalled one focus group that suggested that as a sports car owner, "I really don't care about the passenger, but I want them to think I do."

Vaughan and his team could not take such an approach. They realized that despite the new car's enhanced capabilities, and despite the need for an interior focused on the driver, they could not ignore the second occupant and his or her wants and needs.

Ryan Vaughan was busy with other duties when the initial Stingray interior design blitz was taking place. But when GM Design chief Ed Welburn reopened the competition, Vaughan submitted his ideas for the car's driver and passenger compartment.

Vaughan's theme was selected for development. This illustration shows where he had taken the interior theme and details by June, 2010.

"We understood the occupant package," Vaughan said of the work facing his interior team. "It was going to be fairly similar to today's [C6] car: a big center tunnel that really dominates the interior and sets up much of what you can do.

"We also knew we'd have a touchscreen for the center stack and that it had to be pretty vertical so the sunlight didn't wash it out." Care also had to be taken, he said, so the big screen would remain clearly visible to both the driver and the passenger, even through sunglasses.

But within those restrictions, Vaughan said, "the theme was really up for grabs." (Speaking of grabbing, the seventh-generation Corvette includes a new interior feature: a grab handle to the left of the passenger's seat.)

"We sent the designers to the track before we started the project," said chief engineer Tadge Juechter, "to make sure they knew this cockpit could be a high-stress working environment."

Bennion picks up from there as he tells the handle's story: "We were doing some track events with the [design] program team," he said. "The interior designer got to ride along with a pro driver. Ryan's over six-foot and about two hundred pounds, and all he had was the little door handle to hold on to. It wasn't enough. He came back and designed dual grips."

ASYMMETRICAL SYMMETRY

Don't worry—Vaughan and his interior design team didn't forget the Corvette driver's unique needs when it comes to pushing the new Stingray to its ultimate dynamic potential. Just one example: the side of the center console against which the driver presses his or her right knee while taking 1G left turns on the racetrack was designed to provide the proper amount of support. The driver doesn't slide around, but remains steady at the wheel—and fast but safe around the track—allowing the driver to go home without bruises at the end of the day.

Such asymmetry may seem unusual in the Corvette, which traditionally has been known for its twin-cockpit interior design theme. But Vaughan said that with the dynamic capabilities of the new Corvette, the cockpit needed to be oriented toward the driver, though at the same time providing everything the passenger might need, within easy reach for those occasions when he or she doesn't need a firm grasp on Vaughan's handy handles.

Another example of paying attention to the non-driving occupant is the placement of the passenger-side HVAC (heat, ventilation, and air conditioning) controls. Instead of mounting them in their typical place on the center console, designers incorporated the controls for passenger-side temperature and the passenger-seat heater into the base of the vent at the far right end of the C7's dashboard.

"It's pretty unusual and very expensive," Vaughan acknowledged. But it not only gives the passenger control of his or her environment, it also minimizes the number of controls on the center console.

Also making the interior more comfortable and expensive is the use of Aerogel insulation along the sides and top of the center tunnel, in which the exhaust pipes are now fully enclosed. To control both noise and temperature, Corvette engineers opted for Aerogel, a product proclaimed as the world's lightest solid and sometimes known as "frozen smoke." Aerogel was developed for aerospace use. It is 99.8% empty space and semi-transparent, but because of its insulating properties it is used in things such as the suits astronauts wear.

In the Corvette, in addition to insulating the interior from the high temperature in the tunnel, it also allows beverages and even smartphones to remain cool when stored in the C7 cupholders or center console.

"Doing an asymmetric interior is so much more work," Vaughan said, pointing out that each of the air vents in the Corvette's dashboard is unique. But that's in keeping with the car's overall theme of functional driving design and with challenging the designers to ensure that these diverse parts come together in a way that is pleasing both functionally and aesthetically.

"We used the same process for every piece of the interior," Vaughan said, adding that there were sketch blitzes for many of those components, including the seats, steering wheel, shifter knob, instrument cluster—even the interior trim!—all done to find the best possible solution to achieving the goals for the car's interior.

Complicating that work was the car's inherent dual nature: on one hand a comfortable daily driver and cross-country road-trip vehicle with nearly 30 miles per gallon of fuel economy, and on the other hand a car fully capable of all-out dynamic performance on a weekend at the racetrack or autocross course.

PREPPING THE COCKPIT

One of the challenges for Vaughan and his team was finding a way to meet the needs of all Corvette drivers. Among their solutions was offering drivers their choice of two factory-installed seating platforms. "The seats were a big transformation, a way to push this forward," Vaughan said of the Stingray's interior design.

"Reading the auto reviews, people want a super-aggressive seat for the track, but for everyday driving, that's not necessarily what you need. So we're offering two seats: a [GT] seat—a nice, all-around sports car seat—and a [competition] sport seat that's very track focused. But even the touring seat has more stiffness, a magnesium frame that is much stiffer [than the frame used in previous Corvettes]." The stiff magnesium frame not only saves weight, but also enables the use of seat-mounted side airbags without having to make the seats themselves wider and bulky.

In addition to supplying the taller thigh and body-side bolsters that drivers need for the dynamic forces involved in track-day driving, the Stingray's competition sport seats have a pair of pass-through slots just above the shoulders, just like those in all-out, specially crafted racing seats, which are built to secure the driver with the special five-point safety harnesses required by motorsports sanctioning bodies. Vaughan notes that the shoulder bezels in the Stingray sports seats are made from carbon fiber, not just plastic with a faux-carbon finish.

And, he adds, even the touring seats include a metallic Corvette emblem set in the seat back. Developing such functional yet "really cool" details was part of the interior design team's mission. "This is a very expensive interior," Vaughan said. "Though we didn't get to the drunken-sailor level, we were spending the money, for sure.

"There was some significant investment in the interior, but it was a very smart decision to make and the difference between 'styling' and 'designing' an interior," said Ed Welburn. "I wouldn't say the result is more expensive [in part, he said, because of cooperation between GM's purchasing staff and the interior component suppliers], but it is richer, more complete. The team worked hard on the details.

"No interior is free," Welburn added. "No interior is 'cheap' -- even if it may look cheap." Welburn said what he likes most about the C7 interior is the sum of its parts.

"There are a lot of cool elements," he said. "The materials are so much better than we've had, but it's really the sum of all the parts. Yes, I like the cluster. Yes, I like that the nav screen retracts and there's storage there. I love the materials. The seats not only are so much better than what we've had in the past but they are beautiful pieces of sculpture. It's the sum of all those parts. The whole harmony of the interior. The functionality. Everything in the right location."

These illustrations show how Ryan Vaughan's interior design evolved from an early sketch (top) to a near-final theme (below).

Above: Every piece of a car has to be designed. Here are two illustrations for proposals for seats for the C7 Corvette.

Below: Just as with exterior body panels, the interior and its various components grow from two- to three-dimensions in clay.

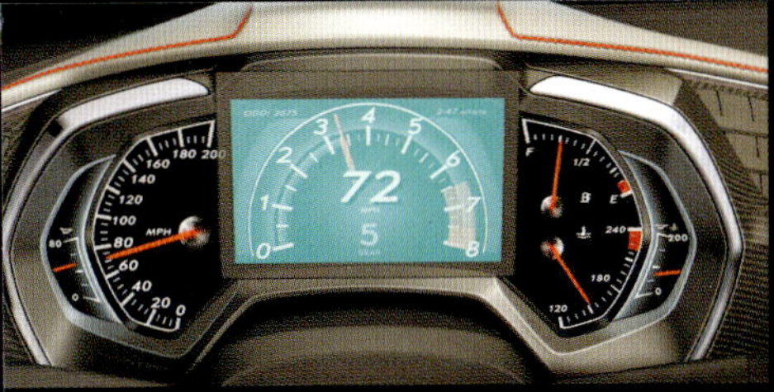

RECONFIGURABLE SCREEN
ANKED BY MECHANICAL GAUGES

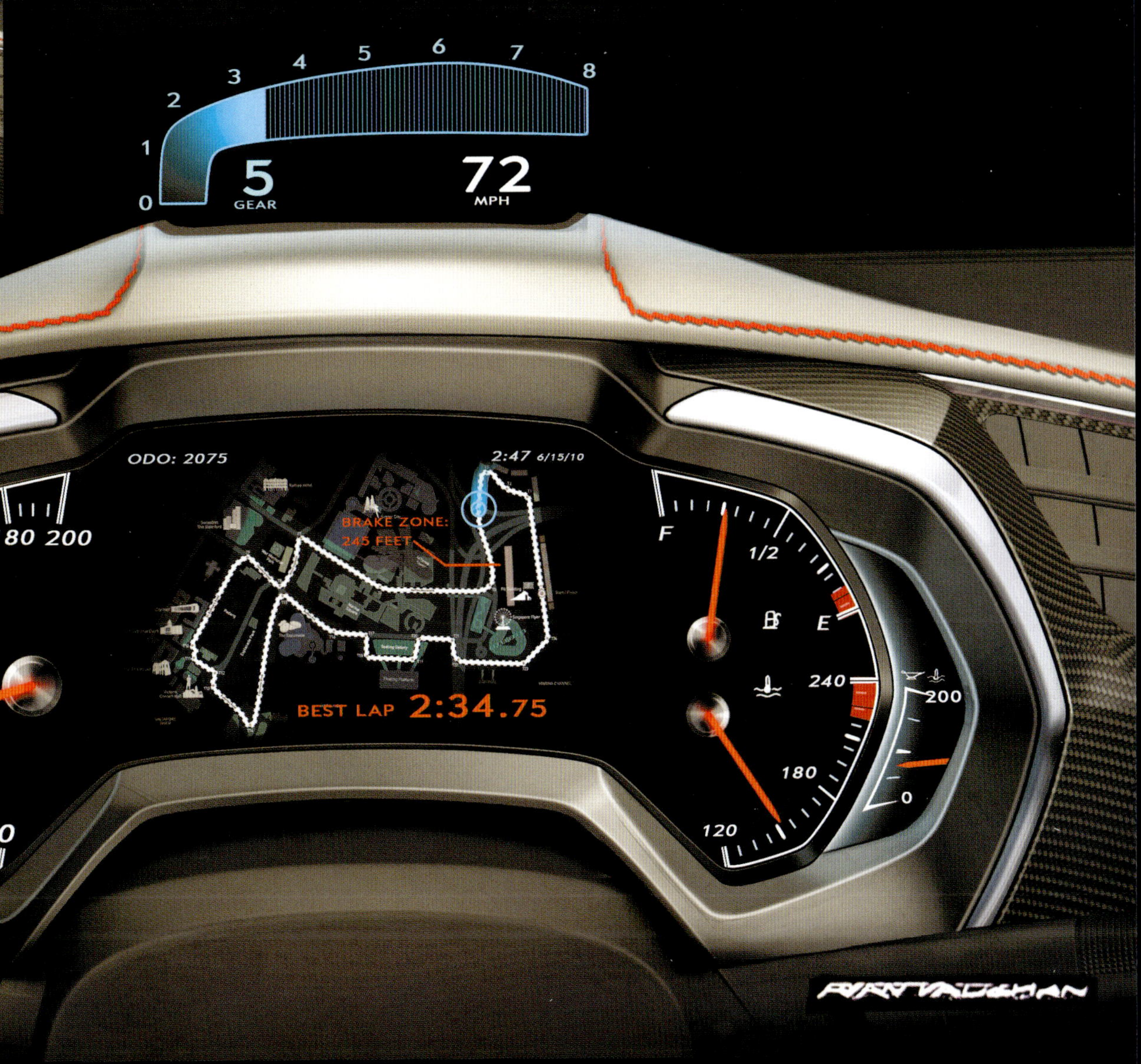

These illustrations show Ryan Vaughan's development ideas for the Corvette's steering wheel, instrument panel and interior door panels.

Ryan Vaughan (left) works with sculptors as the C7 Corvette interior buck begins to take shape.

Just as with the car's exterior theme and details, a full-scale model of the C7 Corvette interior is created to bring two-dimensional drawings into three-dimensional form.

"We wanted to make sure everything was natural, made with authentic materials. We wanted to raise the aspirational level, to give it some more European panache, not to look plasticky. If something looks like aluminum, it really is. If it looks like carbon fiber, it is. But working on a Corvette program [at least in the new General Motors] is unlike anything else. You can ask for leather-wrapping the instrument panel, and they understand. The look, the materials, the technology, the new seats—that was really a big deal.

"And," he added, "it's about us having the confidence not to just emulate other things going on, but going for something unique for Corvette."

While the highly acclaimed interior of the Audi R8 was selected as the benchmark for the execution of the C7 interior in terms of fit and finish and use of materials, Vaughan and his team wanted the cabin to be uniquely Corvette.

For example, in the convertible version of the new Corvette, "we knew we wanted to maintain the waterfall," the area between the seats where, with the top down, it looks as though the body panel cascades from the deck lid into the cockpit, "but to integrate it a little better with the interior trim," Vaughan said.

The new Corvette features a dial to set up the car for various driving environments. And because the instrument panel is basically a large display screen, there are separate cluster displays for touring, sport, and track that use the same bar-graph display as the C6-R racing car. Because the screen is reconfigurable, drivers can further customize the display to meet their personal needs.

In these two photos, the C7 Corvette interior buck takes shape, but note that while the overall theme may be evident—for example, the position of the passenger-side air vents—the details of those vents are yet to be sculpted.

Additional personalization includes such options as suede seating surfaces and an expanded choice of interior colors—Jet Black, Medium Gray, Adrenaline Red, Kalahari, and Brownstone—the latter being what Vaughan described as a "very luxurious" tone that looks as though the entire interior has been dipped in the color.

There was one thing the interior designers wanted but did not get: when equipped with a seven-speed manual transmission, the Stingray will feature new Active Rev Match technology to allow all drivers to do heel-and-toe shifting, blipping the throttle to make sure the engine's RMP count remains consistent. It is a technique racers learn, and it requires using the right foot on the gas and brake pedals at the same time. But Active Rev Match does that for everyone.

What the designers wanted was to have a flip-top ball atop the shift lever. To activate Active Rev Match, the driver would flip open the shifter ball, activate the switchgear, close the ball top, and drive on with Active Rev Match assistance.

"It seemed a natural place," Vaughan said, while admitting that such a device might just be a little too *Bond, James Bond.* And then the engineers pointed out the complexity of such a setup, and the wiring that would be needed to be fit into the stalk itself.

But even then they looked for a solution, though by the time they found one (a supplier that could produce a button that worked with a wireless signal), it was far too late to put into production.

Details begin to emerge on the clay interior model.

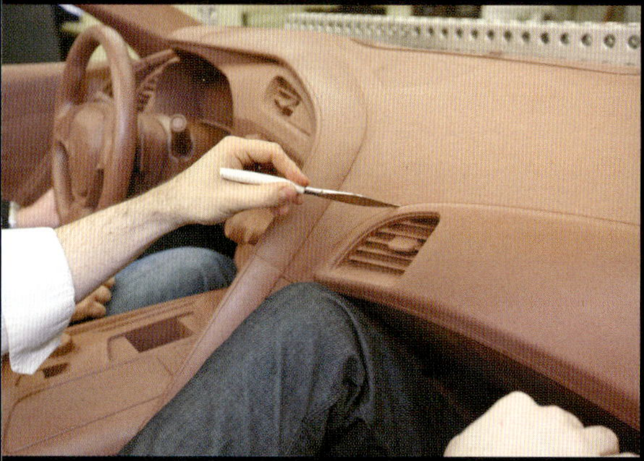

"I love the cockpit shape," Vaughan said. "When you sit in it, the feeling you want as a designer is that you're conveying a feeling and an emotion and that you feel integrated into the car, that the car is wrapped around and tailored to the driver, and that's not easy with different-sized drivers, especially when the package is as tight as it has to be in a car like this."

Getting the look and feel the design team wanted required a new level of integration with those building the car at Bowling Green. "One of the big challenges to complete the cockpit shape is the alignment from the instrument panel to the door," Vaughan said, "especially on the driver's side.

"The first reaction," he remembered, "was 'there's no way' because while it's one thing to align a door skin with the panel itself, what the Corvette interior designers wanted was the alignment of the actual stitching within that transition.

"We brought guys from the [Bowling Green assembly] plant into the studio and told them we were having issues. They said, 'We'll figure out how to it.'"

And they did, even though it means that the trim in the driver's side door panel has to be pivoted into precise location and then locked there with a tool on the assembly line.

"There's no way you could do that on a typical car," Vaughan said. "And as far as I know it's unique in the industry."

But then, so is the Corvette Stingray.

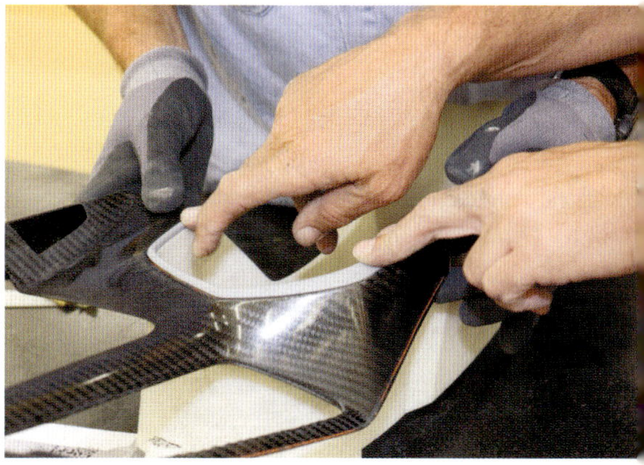

A carbon fiber interior trim panel is readied for installation on the interior clay buck.

This interior buck features a functional "mock-up" shifter to evaluate ergonomics.

CHAPTER 5 ENGINEERING

"How does the race car work better?" Boiled down to its essence, it was a simple question, and one that the engineering strategy for the creation of the seventh-generation Chevrolet Corvette—the 2014 Stingray—would rely upon. The question was posed by Tadge Juechter, the executive chief engineer for the latest version of America's sports car. "Can we apply any of those things to the street?" he wondered.

The goal was to identify technical content and advanced systems that enabled the Corvette Racing team to beat the likes of Ferrari, Porsche, and other competitors, and to apply that technical prowess—in both an aesthetically beautiful, technologically elegant, and financially efficient way—to make the 2014 Corvette even better. The C7 had to appeal not just to the faithful choir of American Corvette enthusiasts, but in a truly global, 21st-century sports car marketplace that already had been evangelized by the car's success in motorsports, especially in the famed 24 Hours of Le Mans, which in most people's minds long ago had supplanted the Indianapolis 500 as the world's most important race.

The Corvette made its debut at Le Mans in 1960, when one of the Chevrolet sports cars entered by America sportsman Briggs Cunningham and driven by American racers John Fitch and Bob Grossman not only won its class but finished seventh overall behind a gaggle of 12-cylinder Ferraris and an Aston Martin DBR1 seemingly identical to one that had won the race the previous year.

DEVELOPMENT

Engineers designing and developing the C7 not only wanted to apply advanced sports car technologies to the new Corvette, they wanted to take advantage of the techniques that the Corvette Racing team used to keep the car ahead of the competition at race tracks around the world.

CORVETTE'S HEAT-ACTIVATED 'SMART MATERIAL'

The new 2014 Chevrolet Corvette uses a lightweight heat-activated shape memory alloy wire in place of a heavier motorized part to open a vent that allows the trunk lid to close more easily.

Owners of the 2014 Corvette Stingray won't be able to see the Active Hatch Vent that makes closing the rear hatch easier, but they'll be able to boast about the use of "smart materials" such as shape memory alloy helps make their cars more energy and mass efficient.

Privately entered Corvettes also won their class in the iconic round-the-clock race in France in 1962, 1969 and 1971. Then, in 2000, an officially backed Corvette Racing team tandem finished third and fourth in the GTS class at Le Mans. A year later, Corvette Racing posted a 1-2 finish in its class, and repeated that feat the following year, then won again in 2004, 2005 and 2006, and again in 2009 and 2011.

The Corvette Racing team also competed in major sports car racing in the United States, where between 2001 and 2012 it won nine manufacturer and eight driver championships.

Though competing in the production-based GT categories, the Corvette Racing team is allowed to make modifications to strengthen the car for competition at top speed and to prepare it for the stress of a 24-hour race. Juechter and his C7 engineering team recognized that some of those techniques and technologies could be used to make their new car better as well.

But they also had their own ideas based on their experiences as sports car development engineers, and the engineering team also was open to ideas from other sources, including the experienced leaders in the General Motors design and product planning departments, and from the companies who supply parts for GM vehicles.

"For us," Juechter said, "it boils down to what makes the car better, and I mean every aspect of the car. We're always thinking about it: If we could do it all over again, what would we do?

"Markets change. Technology advances. What would you do differently?"

Every so often, engineers not only ask such questions, but they get to answer them as they develop the next generation of a particular vehicle. In the case of the C7 Corvette, some of those answers have the racing team looking on in envy.

RACER OR ROCKETSHIP?

In the case of the seventh-generation Chevrolet Corvette, Juechter and his team wanted to do more than just build another new and improved car. They wanted to establish the definition for what they call "modern performance," to build a sports car that provides an enhanced driving experience with more performance *and* more efficiency, and that does so through genuine visible cues—no faux materials or fake aero pieces. Everything on the car would have to justify its function in order to earn its inclusion. Everything would have to contribute to improving the vehicle and to maximizing the experience of the driver or passenger.

A light but strong aluminum frame underpins every seventh-generation Chevrolet Corvette.

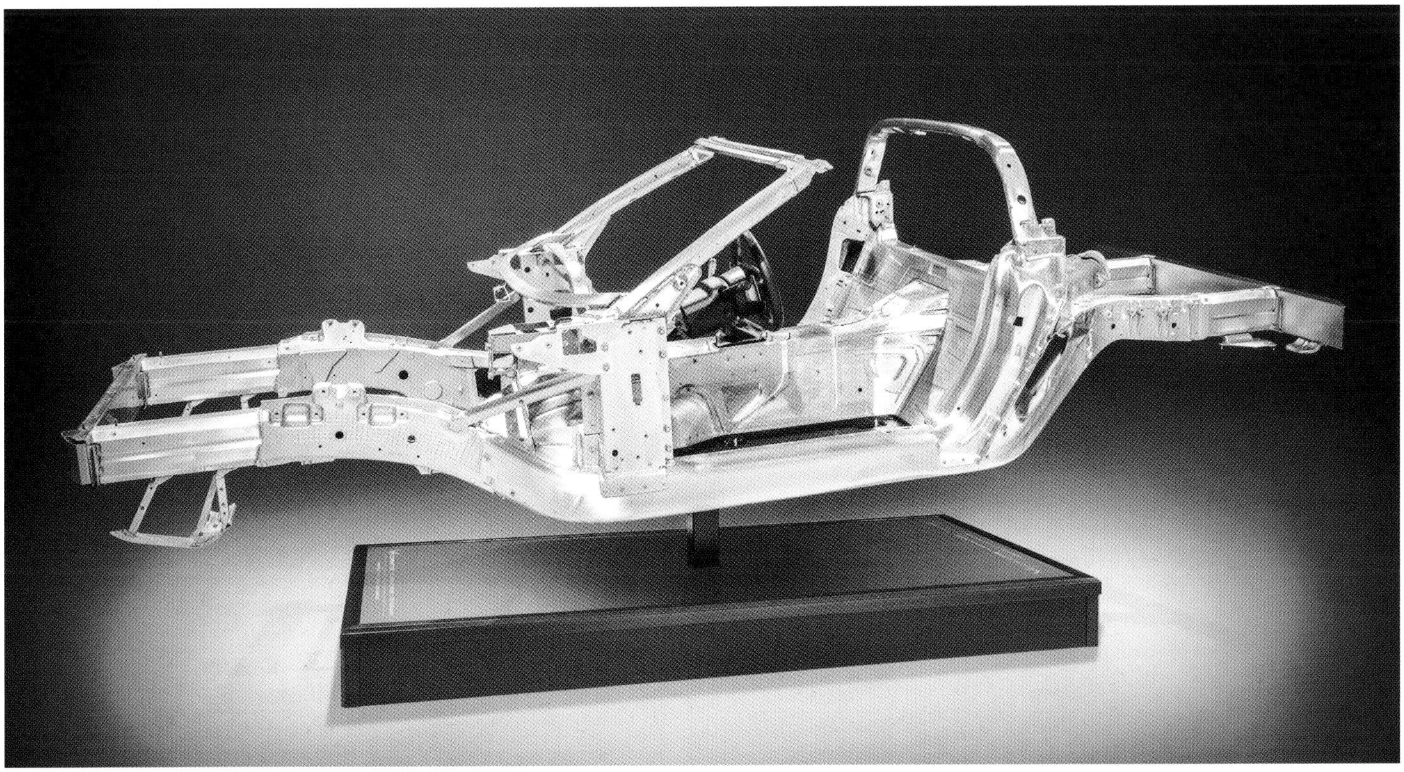

But that meant significant changes. That meant such things as developing two styles of seats to better fit a driver's particular needs (see Chapter 4), and of providing the passenger with a unique environment, from having places to hold on during a particularly spirited ride to positioning passenger-specific climate controls beyond the driver's reach.

The attention to detail—even to seemingly minute nuances—was extraordinary. For example, the new Stingray is equipped with an Active Hatch Vent that car owners will not be able to see, but will appreciate nonetheless. Because the Corvette has a large rear hatch lid over its luggage compartment, but a relatively small and well-sealed passenger compartment, it was necessary to find a way to vent the interior to relieve what engineers call "air bind" that occurs when someone tries to close the hatch.

One solution is simply to ask the car owner to use enough force to slam the hatch shut. Another tactic used on previous Corvettes is to install electric motors to pull the hatch the last inch or so of its travel and to secure the latch that keeps it closed. Yet another solution, again used on previous Corvettes, is a pressure-relief device using thin, rubberized flaps that are forced open by the air pressure as the hatch is closed. None of these solutions has proven optimal (or popular) with vehicle owners.

For the C7 Corvette, engineers have devised another solution, one they feel is technologically advanced yet simple in its execution, and—always a vehicle development goal—one that reduces overall vehicle weight. The solution is the Active Hatch Vent, a device enabled by the creation and development of shape memory alloy.

In the 1960s, the U.S. Navy sought materials that could function in both high temperatures and in extremely corrosive environments. A Naval research lab developed a nickel-titanium alloy and was making a presentation of the material to high-level officers when, as the story goes, one of those officers used a small sample of the alloy to tamp the pipe he'd been smoking. When heated by the smoldering tobacco, the alloy changed its shape and bent. But then it returned to its original shape as it cooled to room temperature, and thus shape memory alloy was discovered. When heated, the crystalline structure within the alloy realigns, thus changing the shape of the metal structure until the source of the heat is removed.

According to Paul Alexander, a Ph.D. and "smart materials" engineer on the C7 Corvette team, General Motors had been experimenting with shape memory alloy for many years. GM saw the potential for using shape memory alloy in automotive applications, but there were issues with obtaining high-quality (durable) material in sufficient supply. "But now we have a supply base," Alexander added, and thus the creation of the Active Hatch Vent for the C7 Corvette.

When the rear hatch is opened, a control module sends an "enable" signal to the Active Hatch Vent, which draws enough electricity for the shape memory alloy to heat enough to change shape, thereby moving a gear that opens vents so air can escape quickly and smoothly as the rear hatch is closed. At that point, the electric charge is shut off, the shape memory alloy returns to its ambient shape, and a spring secures the vents closed.

Made primarily from plastic components and a shape memory alloy wire, the Active Rear Hatch is hidden behind the paneling in the Corvette's cargo compartment. It not only takes up less space than previous solutions, but also eliminates the need for electric motors, solenoids, and special latches, thus reducing overall vehicle mass by as much as 1.3 pounds compared to previous solutions.

While 1.3 pounds may not seem like enough weight to worry the engineers, a pound here and there quickly adds up to significant reductions in mass, thus lightening the load on the engine and therefore saving fuel or opening room for another new component that can contribute to the car's improvement.

The Active Rear Hatch also operates noiselessly and without any electromagnetic interference.

"We're pretty invisible to the customer," Alexander said, adding that while the Active Hatch Vent may be well hidden and operate in silence, it "speaks to the level of detail the Corvette team has tried to bake into everything."

GOODBYE STEEL, HELLO ALUMINUM

While it didn't come from the racing team, shape memory alloy is one only example of the many new technologies embedded into the seventh-generation Corvette. It also is only one example of adding new technologies while subtracting mass.

Just how light is that aluminum frame? Processing engineer Benjamin Hiscox and structures specialist Daniel Trucksis show us.

In the case of the Active Hatch Vent, the weight savings was little more than a pound. But in the case of the C7's new all-aluminum chassis, the weight savings was almost 100 pounds when compared to the former steel frame. And in the case of the chassis, lighter also became stronger—the aluminum chassis is nearly 60 percent more structurally rigid than the steel and aluminum frame used in the previous version of the car.

Juechter said creating a new chassis starts, fittingly, with the "Genesis program," software that "can fabricate a structure out of nothing," as he put it. "You start with a big block of space that the car is going to be inside," he said. Then you carve out space where various components need to be (or where design engineers would like them to be).

"You create negative space and put loads on it and the program synthesizes what the optional structure is," he said. "You get very organized structures, like you see in nature. It looks like roots growing. We are able to take that program that creates the optimum load pass and break that into real parts that we can weld or join together," and modify as needed based on dynamic testing, crash performance, and validation procedures.

"To us engineers, this is the most beautiful part of the car," Juechter said of the chassis. "It's really a beautiful piece of engineering.

"We've completely re-engineered this hydroform frame, optimized it for the best the aluminum industry has to offer, both in parts manufacturing and materials-joining technology."

Hydroforming is a metal-shaping technique that uses water pressure to produce a long and uniform tubular section that is strong and lightweight. "At the C5 intro, we talked about hydroforming as a paradigm-breaking technology. And it is great," Juechter said. "But its downside is that you have the same material thickness everywhere around the length of a section and the material properties have to be the same throughout. You cannot tailor where to use high[er]-strength or extra thickness."

For the frame of the C7 Corvette, however, new aluminum-fastening technologies and other advances in metallurgy and manufacturing allowed Juechter's team to augment the Corvette frame's hydroformed aluminum rail sections with "the strongest you can set," he said of the 7000-series aluminum extrusions designed, for example, to absorb energy in a frontal collision.

"We've kept hydroforming where it makes sense," Juechter said, "for example, throughout the central part of the car." But by using strong and carefully designed 7000-series extrusions, "it takes weight off the front of the car.

"Today's car [the C6] is just slightly nose-heavy, so we did a bunch of things to shift the weight a little to the rear [on the C7]. It helps appearance and puts content centered over the rear wheels. It's now slightly rear-biased, like a race car. We also moved the front wheels forward a little [one inch] to subtly improve the load on those rear tires so they get more traction at launch."

Ed Moss was the engineering group manager for structure on the C7 development team. He said the big challenge was doing one frame for both the coupe and convertible, but adds that since the roof panel above the coupe can be removed, all new Corvettes are actually open-top sports cars.

Moving the front wheels, he said, not only improved weight distribution but was an enabler for those doing the exterior design of the new car while also providing more space beneath the hood for the new small-block engine and auxiliary systems while preserving "crush space" at the front of the car.

Creating an all-aluminum frame wasn't an entirely new experience for Corvette engineers. They had done aluminum frames to lighten and to enhance the dynamic performance of the Z06 and ZR1 versions of the C6. But, said Ed Moss, Corvette engineering group manager for structure, to achieve rigidity goals, that high-performance C6 frame needed an integrated roof panel. For the C7, he said, "we wanted to offer an aluminum frame and a convertible. That was a real challenge."

Because the new frame is so strong, the C7 convertible does not need additional support to make up for its lack of a structural overhead section. In fact, even the coupe version of the C7 features a removable overhead panel, so all StingRay owners can enjoy an open-air driving experience.

Moss was recruited to General Motors in 1988 to do structural analysis of the chassis beneath the fourth-generation Corvette and to help improve the underpinnings beneath the C5 generation. While the chassis for the C5 and C6 cars "is still very efficient for this kind of car," he said, the goal for the C7 was to be lighter and stronger, and to provide for a convertible without having to add structure beneath the open roof.

Initial computer engineering analysis indicated that an aluminum frame could be just as strong as the previous steel chassis. "But why not go up?" Moss and the engineers wondered. So they did—they achieved nearly 60 percent more rigidity than could be employed on the C6.

To create a stronger and lighter frame, the engineers not only tailored the various sections (16 different thicknesses of various grades of aluminum, ranging in thickness from 11 to less than 2 millimeters), but used price shaping in some areas; two octagonal sections are linked like a figure 8, or what Juechter calls a "double bee hive" to enhance strength and energy absorption in the event of an impact.

And to achieve their structural goals, the engineers also had to work with the manufacturing team to explore and implement a variety of metal-fastening technologies, some of which they pretty much had to invent (see Chapter XXX for more about the innovations of the Bowling Green manufacturing plant).

LOSING LIFT AND DOMINANT DOWNFORCE

In addition to being stronger and lighter, the new frame was designed with aerodynamic efficiency in mind. While the frame itself is enveloped within the Corvette's bodywork, its design not only affects the shape of that body, but the internal airflow and ducting needed for cooling the engine, brakes, transmission, differential, and other components, and for efficiently—and smoothly—exhausting that air after it has served its purpose.

And while engineers want the body to fit as tightly as is efficient around the frame and cockpit, they also need room beneath that bodywork for electrical systems, including yards and yards of wiring, and for plumbing fixtures for everything from the fuel system to various coolants and even fresh and air-conditioned ducting for the driver and passenger.

"We've taken the racing solution, which is done in a brute-force sort of way, and integrated it elegantly into a production solution," Juechter said. "It's not just tacked on."

Working with Corvette Racing's own engineering staff, the C7 team devised ways to enhance airflow around and within the car to improve both fuel economy on the highway and top-speed dynamics on the race track, all the while also improving cooling of vital components.

Borrowing technology from the Corvette Racing team, C7 development engineers took much of the air drawn into the front of the car to cool the engine and exhausted it through functional vents in the hood so it flowed over the car's roof, producing downforce that enhances the Stingray's high-speed stability.

Everything from the gear shift to the seatbacks has been meticulously engineered to enhance the driving experience.

Juechter said the Pratt & Miller racing team has done a lot of work with computational fluid dynamics software, and the C7 team used the same modeling techniques to develop aero and air (and liquids) flow for the Stingray.

To reduce frontal surface area that creates drag as the car moves along the road or race track—consuming energy not only to turn the wheels and run onboard systems but to plow through the air—the racing team tilts the radiator (a.k.a. heat exchanger) that cools the engine. And rather than install extra radiators at the front to cool rear-mounted components such as the transmission cooler, the team moves those heat exchangers to the rear of the car and cuts NACA vents into the rear fenders to supply those radiators with cooling air. There also are ducts for cooling the brakes.

Furthermore, to reduce lift at the front of the car—which can become a significant problem when traveling at high speeds—the racers exhaust air through the hood and over the car's roof and rear deck, thus creating stabilizing downforce rather than lift.

For the Stingray, Juechter's engineering team adapted and modified many of those motorsports solutions.

"Our aerodynamics integrates racing strategies from the C6R," Juechter said, noting that the radiator in the C7 is tilted forward and that one third of that air that passes through isn't exhausted beneath the car but through a functional vent on the hood and is guided to flow tightly over the car, creating downforce to stick the car to the pavement.

"The biggest paradigm shift has been for [overcoming] front lift," Juechter said.

"It helps provide downforce and pins the nose of the car, which is a very challenging thing to do on a street car," he said, adding that the usual solution used on a high-performance road car is to bolt on a large lower front lip spoiler or racing-style "splitter." But he said, "those are hell on speed bumps."

While the Corvette has had a rear-mounted transmission as well as differential for many years, coolant for those components was pumped back from the front of the car. "That costs money and it's mass and there's potential for fluid leaks," Juechter said. "Why not use the race car solution? A closed loop system [contained within the rear section of the car] and get a dramatic design element as well?"

For the C7, smaller heat exchangers for the transmission and differential are mounted at the rear and what may become iconic vents are cut into the rear fenders of the Stingray coupe (they are not used on the convertible because of the packaging of the motors needed to raise and lower the convertible top).

Again like the racing team, the C7 engineers and designers created special air intake vents in the Stingray's rear quarterpanels to provide air to cool rear-mounted components such as the transmission and differential radiators. This air vents out around the tail lamps.

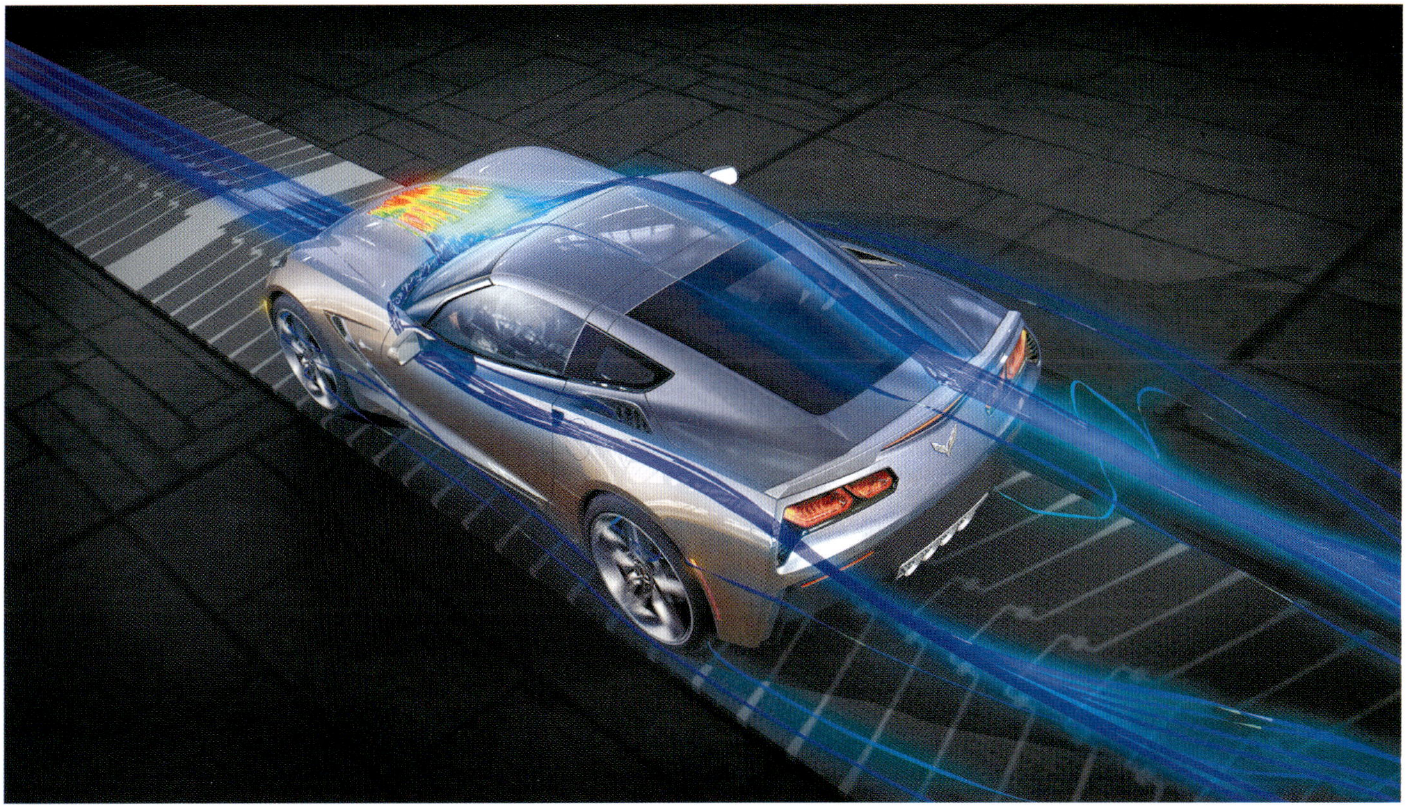

John Bednarchik was the engineer charged with making sure the C7 Corvette had optimized aerodynamics, which means controlling airflow around, over and beneath the car, as well as through the various vents in the car's body. Bednarchik said fine-tuning the C7 consumed more than triple the time a typical GM vehicle spends in the wind tunnel.

Not only were those rear vents carefully designed and engineered in the wind tunnel, they are signature aesthetic elements in the design. Also elegant is the solution of releasing the spent air from the rear of the car through vents around the tail lamps and through additional vents in the lower rear fascia.

"That we were able to achieve all these things is a really big deal," said John Bednarchik, C7 aerodynamics performance engineer who worked on turbine engines. Bednarchik worked on aero/thermal development at Chrysler before joining General Motors in the late 1980s.

At first, Bednarchik said, he was assigned to GM Powertrain doing cooling and HVAC (heating/ventilation/air conditioning) development and testing "while waiting for someone in the aero group to retire." That happened in time for him to be part of the team that designed and developed the C6 and now the C7 Corvettes.

Even with the racing team's help and all of the computational fluid dynamics work, he added, the C7 team spent more than 700 hours in the General Motors wind tunnel fine-tuning aerodynamics and the flow and dissipation of air for the various radiators and brakes. By the way, 700 hours is more than *triple* the time scheduled for a typical production car program, and even some 200 hours more were used to stretch the efficiency of the Chevrolet Volt electric car.

Much of that time in the tunnel was spent achieving balance between the conflicting demands for reducing drag while also keeping the car and its internal components cool, not to mention the conflicting desires of design aesthetics and engineering functionality. Furthermore, the location of air ducts had to be optimized (though much of the work on cooling was accomplished through CFD studies before the car was in the tunnel).

Nonetheless, there were issues such as the design of the mesh and the spacial relation between that mesh and the louvers within the rear fender vents that had to be tested, altered, retested, and validated. It was the same with the exit vents around the tail lamps and the lower rear fascia.

And Bednarchik probably could write an entire engineering dissertation on the work it takes to balance the aerodynamic efficiency of the front corner of the car while meeting the latest government standards for providing protection for a pedestrian who might bump into a fender.

Bednarchik also notes that only a third of the air flows over the car from beneath the hood because the rest is required to help keep what he calls the "big thermal-generating device" (the small-block V-8) at optimum operating temperature.

A CORVETTE THAT (ALMOST) FLOATS

Covering the chassis and guiding air for downforce and cooling is the C7's composite body.

When Corvette production began, the bodywork was made from fiberglass. But that has evolved over the years. For the C7, most body panels will be a carbon nano hybrid of carbon fiber and glass fiber, with a carbon fiber hood and removable roof panel.

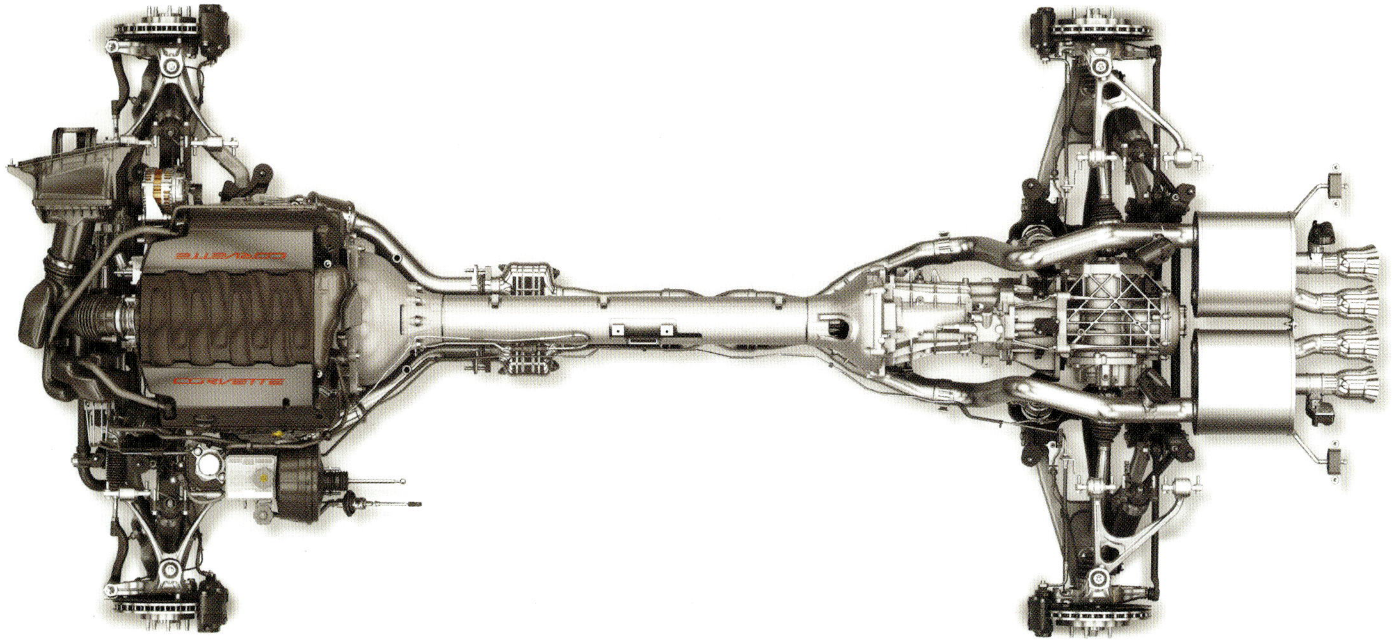

Front and rear cradles carry components such as the engine, transmission, differential, and suspension, including the wheels, tires, and brakes. Like the C7 frame, the cradles are made from lightweight but strong aluminum.

Robert Morrison, founder of the Molded Fiber Glass Companies of Ashtabula, Ohio, long ago earned a place in the Corvette Museum and Hall of Fame for his company's work.

"They've been on the car since 1953," said Moss. "I applaud them for their work on chemistry and doing the carbon nano panels."

Moss explained that because of that chemistry—the clay resin in the panels is more spherical and has better bonding qualities—the new body panels, made with 15 percent carbon content and 30 percent glass fibers, are not only stronger, but 20 percent lighter as well.

In fact, Moss said, the new panels have a specific gravity of 1.2. Water has a specific gravity of 1.0.

"We're getting very close to having our composite panels float in water," Moss said.

"We have a lot of carbon in this car," Juechter added. "There's no car in this price range, there's no car even close that offers this much."

Carbon fiber is four times lighter but 10 times stronger than steel. The carbon fiber hood and roof panel on the C7 reduce vehicle weight by 17 pounds versus the traditional fiber glass components. However, carbon fiber also is very expensive in terms of raw materials and production costs, and its use has been focused on products where performance trumps cost. A few of those products include your everyday jet fighters, grand prix racing cars, and uber-expensive sports cars.

But the Corvette designers and engineers have taken advantage of new technologies that are making carbon fiber components less expensive.

WHEELING AND DEALING

Another change to the chassis structure of the C7 is the use of hollow-cast front and rear "cradles," the components which hold the engine and transmission, and to which suspension components are attached. Previously, sold aluminum was used for such cradles. Advances in casting techniques, however, have produced hollow components that not only are lighter, but 20 percent stiffer.

Hollow lower control arms also are used in the new car's front and rear suspension. Again, they improve stiffness and suspension response but reduce overall vehicle weight by nearly nine pounds.

Attached to the suspension are new "directional" wheels, 18 inches in diameter on the front axle, and 19 inches across at the rear. The five-spoke wheels are "directional" because as the spokes meet the wheel hub, they are slightly angled in the direction of forward travel.

"There's a little directionality applied where the spokes tend to intersect the hub," said designer Kirk Bennion. "We haven't had anything like that on Corvette . . . five-spoke is a good footprint, but having a little bit of directionality is also good." And inside those wheels are Brembo-brand brakes with four-piston fixed calipers (instead of the previous sliding calipers).

"Basically you've got bigger rotors, more pad surface area and more pistons for additional braking force," said Mike Bailey, C7 vehicle systems engineer for chassis. "From a track perspective, you're going to have less fade, improved modulation, and reduced drag."

Juechter added that the swept area is 35 percent greater than on the C6, and said that stopping distances should decrease by 9 percent, or some 11 feet when decelerating from 60 miles per hour.

A set of Michelin Pilot Super Sport tires will be wrapped around the new wheels. This is another change that traces directly to the Corvette Racing Team (refer to Chapter 2 for details).

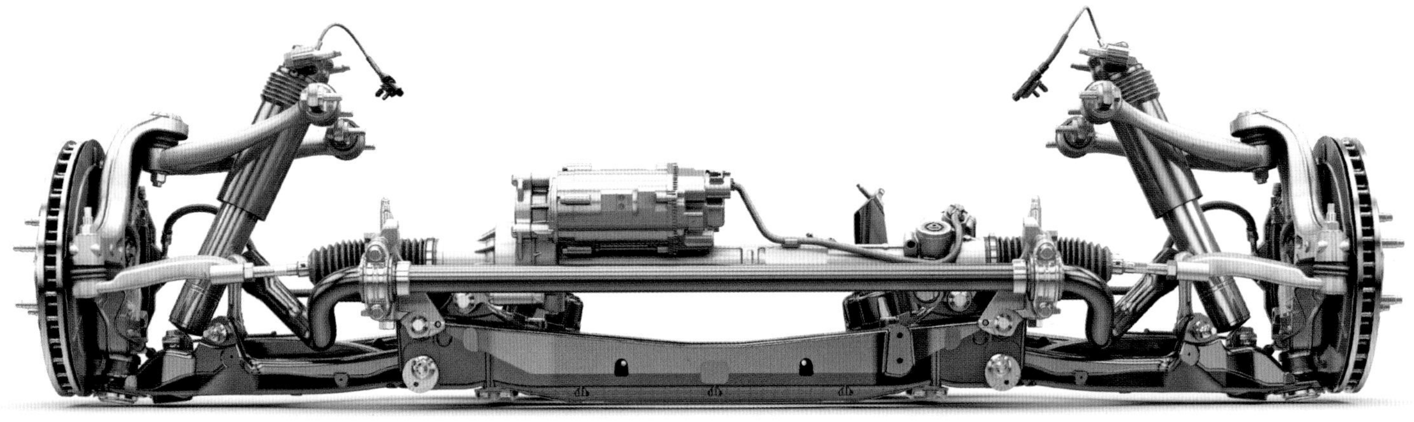

For drivers who want to push beyond the restrictions encountered (and enforced) on public roads, the Corvette engineering team developed an optional Z51 Performance Package.

According to Juechter, the Z51 is a track-certified car out of the factory. While engine output is the same, dry sump lubrication (an oil reservoir separate from the oil pan) is used to assure proper lubrication during the high g-forces encountered on the race track. The manual transmission has performance ratios designed for track use, and cars with automatic transmissions get a more aggressive final drive. The Z51 package also includes a transmission cooler, larger wheels (19 inches in front and 20 at the rear) and brakes, and an Electronic Limited Slip Differential. The Generation-3 Magnetic Ride Control system is also available with the Z51 package.

The new and third-generation of Magnetic Ride Control replaces the conventional shock absorbers with electronically controlled units filled with a magneto-rheological (MR) fluid in which tiny iron particles are suspended. Sensors constantly "read" the vehicle/road interface and interaction and within 15 milliseconds (40 percent faster than previous generations), a magnetic charge aligns the iron particles to provide real-time damping and more precise body control, but with a comfortable ride for non-track travel.

Wheels have split-spoke architecture and are 19 inches up front and 20 across at the rear. Front brake discs are an inch larger in diameter (13.6 inches). The discs

also are slotted for better cooling and have lighter weight dual casting tips on the front wheels. Juechter said braking is 5-percent better than on the heralded Grand Sport version of the C6 Corvette.

The electronic limited-slip differential (eLSD) is a hydraulically-actuated clutch designed to adjust the torque split between the drive wheels from open (unlocked) to full engagement—from 0 to 2,000 Newton meters of torque—within 200 milliseconds (0.2 seconds), or about half the time it takes to blink your eyes. But eLSD is not merely on or off; it's continuously variable and designed to optimize the torque split between the rear wheels for enhanced traction and power delivery.

The technology originally was developed at GM for use on a 300-horsepower, ultra-high performance version of the front-drive Chevrolet Cobalt, a car that ultimately did not go into production. The Corvette is the first rear-drive sports car to be equipped with such technology, and it had to be designed to be particularly robust because of the car's dynamic potential.

"Our torque-vectoring unit is the driver's right foot," explained Alex McDonald, C7 performance integration engineer. "With the eLSD, the aspects that enable that to be the best technology for Corvette is the car's low center of gravity and the car's width. Our inside-rear wheel is always doing something, even at maximum lateral g, and the throttle pedal can almost overwhelm both rear wheels at any time. ELSD is the most effective and mass-efficient way to get the yaw-dampening effect you want. On a sports car chassis, we don't need help getting the car to turn. We use the eLSD to slow that down."

The eLSD reacts based on an algorithm that considers data from many sensors, including vehicle speed, steering input, and throttle position to provide enhanced traction, balanced handling, and improve steering feel for the driver seeking the fastest way around a track. But it also has benefits on the highway, especially in lane-change and emergency maneuvers.

In effect, eLSD provides stability control without having to involve the car's braking system.

"The electronic limited-slip differential transforms the Stingray by optimizing handling for the driving situation," said Mike Bailey, C7 vehicle systems engineer for chassis. "By continuously modulating the torque split between the rear wheels, the eLSD can improve traction accelerating out of corner, improve stability on the highway, and enhance steering turn-in and responsiveness."

McDonald, himself a former sports car racer, notes that because of the rules of racing, the new Stingray can be equipped with technology that isn't allowed on the track.

"The racing team doesn't have the stuff we do—the eLSD and the MR dampers and the traction control. We're going beyond because we don't have the rules they do."

But, he added, "any racing team in the world would kill for an eLSD."

"It makes a night and day difference in vehicle dynamics," Juechter added.

Harlan Charles compares the Driver Mode Selector on the new C7 Corvette to the graphic equalizer used on high-end home audio systems—instead of having to deal with an array of adjustments, the driver simply dials in the anticipated driving conditions, from "Weather" to "Track" and the car's various systems automatically adjust to enhance dynamic performance.

CUSTOMIZING THE DRIVING EXPERIENCE

Further enhancing the Stingray driver's experience are new technologies such as electronic power steering and the Driver Mode Selector.

Electric power steering eliminates the traditional power steering pump and the bleeding of power from the engine to operate that pump. Instead, it uses electronic controls to provide variable ratios, and tailors steering effort for various driving situations. It also negates unwanted road feedback experienced by drivers of high-performance cars, as well as countering the "lead pull" feel felt by those traveling heavily- trafficked roads and freeways in cars with wider tires.

Steering feel is further improved by use of a steering wheel that's 360 millimeters (little more than 14 inches) in diameter, by increasing steering-column stiffness by 150 percent, increasing intermedia steering shaft torsional stiffness by 600 percent, and by mounting the steering gear to the front cradle structure. Added together, C7 steering is five times stiffer than on the C6.

Juechter said he didn't believe that number—five times stiffer!—when he first heard it.

"I asked for proof," he said, "and they showed me the data."

Another aspect of the new steering system is the steering wheel. Juechter noted that the smaller steering wheel "makes the whole car feel smaller" from the driver's perspective. In fact, he said, the diameter has been shrunk to where the wheel is approaching the size of that used in the Corvette Racing cars.

"The trick with a small wheel is getting a good view of the instrument cluster, having room for the redundant controls on the wheel, and shrinking the airbag while still meeting driver safety requirements. It's a big challenge."

But like many other aspects of the new C7, it was a challenge that was met. Another challenge for the engineer team was the Driver Mode Selector—a dial on the center console that lets the driver select from among Weather, Eco, Tour, Sport, and Track modes.

"If you look at the sixth-generation Corvette, where we're getting to the later models, there were a lot of things you [the driver] could control," said Harlan Charles, Corvette product [planning] manager. "We had the magnetic [ride] selector control dial, but we also had other modes for steering (variable ratio and variable effort), electronic throttle control, a dual-mode exhaust system, and the automatic transmission with different modes—firm for performance or smoother, and launch control. And then we added Performance Traction Management, which had its own set of modes.

"We had a lot of things you might want to vary or have control over."

Perhaps too many, at least based on the number of control switches fighting for real estate within reach of the driver.

Charles wondered if the automotive equivalent of a graphic equalizer couldn't be created, "where instead of having to adjust everything separately, you just have 'rock' or 'jazz' or 'country.' Let the driver pick what kind of driving you're going to do and then [automatically] adjust all the adjustable attributes of the car to meet those needs."

As if coordinating everything with a single knob wasn't challenging enough, Charles also wondered, since a reconfigurable display screen was going to be used on the instrument panel and atop the center stack, why couldn't the display adjust in response to the mode the driver selected?

Charles' ideas were met with lukewarm interest by the engineering team, but then he a created a spreadsheet-style matrix listing all the various attributes and where they fit on a scale with comfort at one end and race-track aggressiveness at the other.

Instead of having myriad possibilities and permutations, Charles' chart showed that five combinations would span nearly all driving situations.

"There was a logical combination of things," he said, noting, for example, that "why would you want the Magnetic Ride in Touring mode when you're on the track with the steering in Track mode? Why would you do that?"

Charles also realized that by creating five modes, they could be controlled by a single knob, which meant a driver could change modes on the fly rather than having to stop and adjust a variety of knobs and switches. "By making its more streamlined, you're giving the driver more control because they can use it on the fly in the car," Charles said.

Sounds great, right? Of course, it was the engineers who had to figure out a way to make it all work, which could be complicated enough, but more so because of the need to coordinate across disciplines.

"But this was something we identified from Day 1 of the program, from the beginning," Charles said, adding that the attitude became that of working together, even across the usual lines of demarcation between design and engineering. "We still had a lot of debate about what should be in what mode, and what attributes might be shared [in multiple modes]," Charles said.

But, he added, despite the need to write pages and pages of computer codes and tables, engineers realized that the Driver Mode Selector eliminated complexity and complications for the driver by adjusting and coordinating a dozen "performance parameters": the active exhaust system (which alters the exhaust note based on driving mode); the Active Fuel Management; the active handling (StabiliTrak); the automatic transmission's shift points; the eLSD; the Electronic Throttle Control; the launch control (which provides maximum acceleration from a standing start); the Magnetic Ride Control; the Performance Traction Management system; the electronic steering; the traction control; and even the gauge cluster configuration.

And what excites Charles the most is the way the gauge cluster reflects the selected mode. For example, in Tour mode you see traditional gauges, though presented in a modern or even futuristic graphic design, as well as turn-by-turn navigation information.

For Sport mode, he said, "we kept the classic Corvette gauges you'd expect."

But opt for Track and the dashboard looks like that in the C6.R racing cars, with read outs for lap times and shift lights across the top to help the driver extract maximum performance. There's even a "friction bubble" to show dynamic performance parameters.

The HUD (heads-up display) projects vehicle speed and other parameters onto the windshield so the driver can see them without looking down at the gauges. It's even reconfigurable.

Alex McDonald, the engineer who did much of the Driver Mode Selector coordination because the codes ultimately reside in his brake control module, said one dividend of the selector setup is enhanced driving in winter weather. A high-performance, rear-drive sports car has inherent challenges on icy or snow-covered surfaces, McDonald acknowledged, but, he added, if you opt for the Weather setting and put a set of Michelin's special winter tires on the car, "you'll forget it's a Corvette."

Even without winter tires, the Stingray features first-time technology that adjusts Driver Mode Selector parameters based on tire temperatures. The system was devised by McDonald and his C6 predecessor, Mike Petrucci.

Not only do the valve stems on modern tires measure a tire's internal air pressure, but also temperatures (though at the valve stem, not at the tread). But by using not just tire valve temperature but other variables, including engine air intake and engine coolant temperatures, McDonald and Petrucci were able to enhance the software that manages anti-lock braking and the eLSD systems based on tire temperatures. There are three ranges—less than 45 degrees, between 45 and 115 degrees, and more than 115 degrees.

One benefit of the patented Tire Temperature System is a reduction by nearly five feet in stopping distance from 60 miles per hour on cold tires. Another temperature-sensitive innovation being introduced on the C7 Stingray is an adjustable redline. At normal operating temperatures, the new small-blcok V-8 has a redline of 6,500 rpm. But when the engine is first started, the redline indicated on the dashboard can be as little as 3,500 rpm. The line then moves across the electronic tach display as the engine reaches optimal temperatures.

The new Corvette, Charles said, gives its owner three cars in one: a long-distance GT car; a car with the connectedness and infotainment capabilities the commuter needs; and the acceleration, grip, and braking for the race track.

"With the Driver Mode Selector, we wanted to give the driver an easy way to tailor virtually every aspect of the car to fit their driving environment," Charles said. "The result is a more rewarding, more confident experience, whether you're commuting in a downpour or charging through the Corkscrew at Laguna Seca."

HEEL AND TOEING: NOT JUST FOR RACERS

Enhancing those lap times at Laguna Seca and other tracks (and improving cornering performance on the street as well) is yet another new C7 technology—Active Rev Match.

Active Rev Match, which allows any driver to execute "heel-and-toe" gear shifts just like a Le Mans racer, is activated by paddles on either side of the steering wheel.

The optimum method for maintaining vehicle speed and stability in a car equipped with a manual transmission is to match the engine crankshaft's rate of revolutions in each gear engaged. But this is often difficult to accomplish because the driver's feet are outnumbered by the pedals that control the clutch, brake, and accelerator.

Successful race car drivers become skilled at what is called "heel and toeing:" by using their right foot on both the accelerator and brake pedals, their left foot can engage the clutch pedal. For example, as a racer prepares for a turn, the right toe depresses the brake pedal to slow the car while the right heel keeps enough pressure on the accelerator to maintain the desired vehicle speed. Just as a gear shift is being made, the driver's right heel quickly presses or blips the throttle so the engine speed—the rpm indicated on the tachometer—are the same in the new gear as they were in the previous gear.

But all drivers of the manually shifted C7 Corvettes will be able to duplicate this feat because the car's new seven-speed manual transmission has "smart" technology, an algorithm that tracks engine and transmission data and blips the throttle for the driver to match rpm on upshifts and downshifts.

The Active Rev Match is activated by a paddle on the steering wheel and functions at speed of 10 miles per hour or more.

PAST AND FUTURE

From Active Hatch Vent and Active Rev Match and from its new chassis to its Driver Mode Selector and other new technologies, "the car has dramatically upgraded in every aspect," said Juechter.

"Corvette is a car that can't be done like a normal car," he added. "You have to have better synthesis between engineering, design, marketing, and purchasing. Chevrolet has more than 100 years of history with structure and a lot of regimented processes on how you do things. [But] Corvettes come along every decade or so and are completely unregimented. The design is completely different; the way they're assembled is completely different.

"We've taken the strengths of Corvette and made them even better while not walking away from who we are. We looked at how we could make it more comfortable and improve performance, and what kind of technology can break the paradigm to give you more fuel-efficiency and faster zero-to-sixth times. We respected our heritage, but at the same time moved into the future."

The all-new 2014 Chevrolet Corvette Stingray's provocative exterior styling is as functional as it is elegant; every line, vent, inlet and surface has been optimized to enhance the car's overall performance.

CHAPTER

6

THE NEW SMALL-

Chief engineer Tadge Juechter enjoys opening a briefcase and showing off the only two small parts that carry over from the sixth- to the seventh-generation Corvette, and Jordan Lee has his own version of that show. Lee is the global chief engineer and program manager for Chevrolet's "small-block" V-8 engines. A new and fifth-generation small-block will empower the 2014 Corvette. Lee likes to point out that only the "starter bolts, piston pin, pin clip, and valve retainer and keeper" have been retained from the previous small-block V-8.

"Everything else," he says, "is new."

And yet this new and fifth-generation small-block still traces a direct heritage back to the original and revolutionary Chevrolet small-block introduced for the 1955 model year. "The small-block is the only engine I know of with an unbroken lineage since 1955," Lee said, explaining that the engine's lineage is built around the layout of a 90-degree "V" with cylinder bore centers spaced 4.4 inches apart on each bank with a two-valves-per-cylinder architecture.

BLOCK V-8

The new Gen5 Small-Block V-8 is manufactured at Chevrolet's Tonawanda engine plant.

A new fifth-generation of Chevrolet small-block V-8 engines powers the new Chevrolet Corvette Stingray.

But can an architecture created nearly 60 years earlier still be applicable and effective in a sports car created for a 21st Century global driving environment?

The original Chevy small-block displaced 265 cubic inches (4.3 liters) and produced 195 horsepower when topped by a four-barrel Rochester carburetor in the 1955 Corvette. The new and fifth-generation small-block is a 6.2-liter V-8 that provides up to 460 horsepower to the 2014 Stingray. Equipped with this engine—and with the engine linked to a technologically advanced seven-speed manual or six-speed automatic transmission—the 2014 Stingray is capable of attaining speeds approaching 200 miles per hour on a race track, but also of traveling nearly 30 miles of public highway while consuming a single gallon of unleaded gasoline.

"Each generation grows and improves," Lee said of the small-block engine's development through five technological generations.

While the basic architecture has been retained throughout the engine's history, the internal changes can be seen as revolutionary rather than evolutionary, and that's especially the case with the new Generation-5 Chevy small-block, which uses direct injection, continuously variable valve timing, and cylinder deactivation, which General Motors calls Active Fuel Management, to provide both power and fuel economy.

"This is the most revolutionary change of the small-bock engine in its 57-year history, Lee said, "it's not just a refresh of an old architecture. We took a beloved engine and used the latest tools and technology to redefine and re-optimize every component and system to keep it class-leading in every aspect that is relevant for today's environment. This means exceptional power, torque, fuel efficiency, durability, and very low noise."

Indeed. Chevrolet likes to point out that the new and Generation-5 small-block features technology unavailable on the engines of more expensive sports cars produced in Germany and Italy—in some cases *much* more expensive—than the new Stingray.

ALL THE PRETTY HORSES

The original 1953 Corvette carried Chevrolet's venerable Blue Flame—an inline six-cylinder engine—beneath its hood. When used in Chevrolet sedans, the engine was rated at a little more than 100 horsepower. For the Corvette, and equipped with a trio of side-draft carburetors, the engine was rated at 150 horsepower—an impressive figure for the early 1950s, and only 10 horsepower less than the six-cylinder used in the Jaguar XK-120. At the same time, however, the six-cylinder engine in the C-type racing version of the Jaguar was producing 200 horsepower and Ferrari's V12 was pumping out 300 horses.

Ed Cole, the engineer who had led the development of a new V-8 for post-war Cadillacs, was managing an assembly plant in Ohio when Chevrolet invited him back to Michigan to create a new and compact V-8 engine. The engine Cole designed was elegant in simplicity, small in size and weight, but powerful nonetheless, producing 195 horsepower. The engine made its public debut in the Corvette that served as the pace car for the 1955 Indianapolis 500 and soon was racing down the beach at Daytona and up Pikes Peak in the famous "Climb to the Clouds" race. Nearly everyone who bought a 1955 Corvette—more than 690 of the 700 produced—ordered the V-8 engine.

Every 1956 Corvette carried a small-block V-8 (now with higher compression and a new carburetor) and rated at more than 200 horsepower. For 1957, the engine was offered with fuel injection that boosted performance to 283 horsepower. The small-block was so versatile that displacement and horsepower could be modified for various needs, ranging from more efficiency to meet global fuel supply crises, federal emission legislation, and the use of non-leaded fuels in the

1970s, to the special and unique demands of stock car, sports, and pony car racing.

Typically, however, displacement and power increased through the years, eventually reaching 5.7 liters and 375 horsepower in standard production guise. A second-generation small-block launched in the early 1980s. A third-generation V-8 arrived more than a decade later and provided more than 400 horsepower for the C5 Corvette. A fourth-generation small-block, both more powerful and more fuel efficient, was introduced for the 2005 model year.

Though many may see the Chevy small-block as an old-school engine that lacks such modern mechanical components as double-overhead camshafts, GM Powertrain engineers like to talk about *power density*. Power density refers to

This cutaway shows the inner workings of the fifth-generation small-block V-8.

how the small-block provides outstanding performance when measured by horsepower per kilogram of engine mass—as much as 2.59 hp/kg when the 6.2-liter LS9 (a Generation-4 small-block) was supercharged—and yet also provides astounding fuel economy. The C6 Corvette cruised highways at 26 miles per gallon. "Fuel efficiency is not the reason you buy a Corvette," said John Rydzewski, the assistant chief engineer for small-block development. "But once you do, you brag about it."

"For some customers, for example, those who own an SUV or a big sedan," said Corvette chief engineer Tadge Juechter, "the Corvette is the economy car in their personal fleet."

The Corvette can often be seen as an economy car because, as GM designers will tell you, the engine is so compact. A compact engine enables the Corvette's iconic long- and low-nosed styling to enhance the car's aerodynamic efficiency while providing the driver with a better view of the road race track ahead. "A Corvette would not look like it does with a twin-turbo, over-head cam engine," Lee said.

Juechter also noted that the new small-block is 40 pounds lighter and four inches shorter in height than a European high-performance automaker's smaller but twin-turbocharged and double-overhead cam V-8.

Small displacement engines (even a V-6) with one or two turbochargers were considered for the C7, but Chevrolet and Powertrain engineers were quickly convinced that such engines could not match a new and technologically advanced small-block in performance or fuel economy.

Lee noted that in addition to the benefits the engineers see in a normally aspirated V-8, Corvette buyers like the instant response the small-block provides. "Tip into the throttle and there's a ground-swell of torque," he said. "Others with boosting devices have made turbo lag better, but they haven't eliminated it. That's a characteristic we wouldn't like in a Corvette, which gives you instant torque and power."

MORE THAN A FUEL SYSTEM

So how do GM Powertrain engineers decide it's time for a new small-block? Lee said that decision can be triggered by emission regulations, competitive reasons, technological advances, or all of the above.

Sometimes, he added, the answer can be a relatively minor refresh during a generation's production run, but sometimes the answer is an all-new engine.

Like the 5th-generation small-block in the C7.

The process, he explained, starts with setting requirements for fuel economy, for power and torque—even the shape of the torque curve—for responsiveness and refinement, even for how loud or quiet the engine should be.

"We start with all of those attributes and then ask which technologies are available," Lee said. "What new analytical tools do we have? What new techniques? We really push the envelope every time we get to do a new engine."

Lee said that each time GM Powertrain contemplates a next-generation small-block, it re-examines the historic small-block architecture to determine if it still provides the optimal solution, and not just for American drivers. They want an answer for what they consider the modern auto industry has become—a truly global driving environment.

"We choose our architecture very carefully," he said. "We're not necessarily trying to carry over the old setup, but that architecture still works. The numbers speak for themselves."

And that architecture not only works, but enables even the newest Corvette to still look like a Corvette.

For the Generation-5 small-block, targets were set in consultation with Tadge Juechter's C7 engineering team, including 450 horsepower and 450 pound-feet of torque—record figures for the basic Corvette. But at the same time, the new engine had to offer reduced emissions and expanded fuel economy, enhanced refinement and responsiveness, and provide the proper aural spectrum from idle through top speed, working for everything from daily commuter driving to dealing with the stress and strain encountered on the race track.

"Doing a new engine is always very exciting," said Lee, a 30-year GM Powertrain veteran who has worked on everything from the Quad 4 to the Northstar, and from experimental engine programs that didn't make it to production to the venerable small-block, which has become GM's basic V-8 engine. The V-8 small-block is used in various forms in everything from pickup trucks to Corvettes.

"The small-block is a huge deal," Lee said. "For me and for my counterparts it's magical. It has such a history, a rich history." And for four years, Lee and his team worked to add to that history through the development of the fifth-generation Chevy small-block.

"Tadge had some strict goals in mind," said Lee. "Zero-to-60, quarter-mile, track targets. Power and torque were at the top of the totem pole," he added. "We want the most powerful engine we can achieve within the [architectural] requirements of the car itself."

Powertrain engineers look at new technologies that can achieve even the most aggressive of targets. For example, increasing the engine's internal compression ratio improves power, torque and fuel efficiency—and all without requiring the use of fuel with premium octane ratings. One way to do that is to employ direct injection technology that injects gasoline directly and precisely into the combustion chamber. Not only does this achieve the goals listed above, but it keeps the combustion chamber cooler, enabling a higher compression ratio and reducing emissions, especially cold-start emissions which are reduced by some 25 percent.

"But it's more than just a fuel system," Lee said. "You can't just add it to the previous-generation engine. You need to modify the cylinder heads, the pistons, and the entire combustion system. You need to move the valves. So you're pretty much into a new engine design.

"This led us to understand that we need to do an all-new engine, and to put

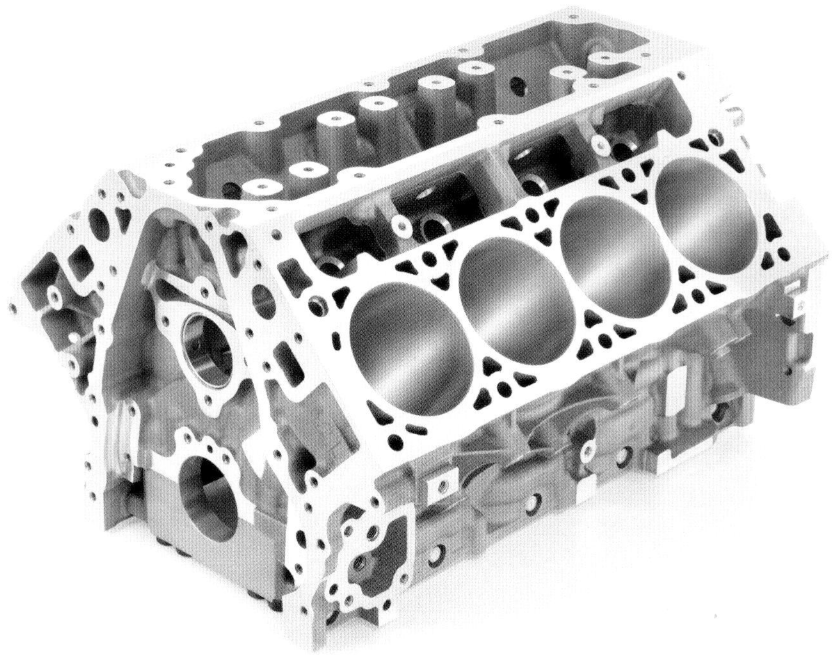

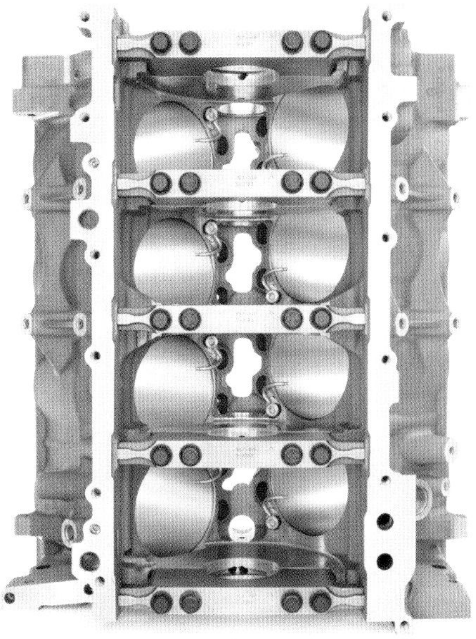

The new Gen-5 small-block V-8 engine block has cast-in cylinder bore liners and main caps with four main bolts as well as two cross bolts per cap. Such a strong bottom end is the foundation for any high-performance engine.

Viewed from beneath, the squirters that apply oil to the backside of the pistons can be seen.

all the refinements and optimizations into it that are available that we didn't have 10 years ago."

Changes include a smaller combustion chamber, unique piston-head topography, and heads with larger, straight and rectangular intake ports designed with a "slight twist" to enhance fuel mixture motion. Swapping the intake and exhaust valve locations allowed the spark plug to be repositioned, placing the electrode closer to the center of the fuel "pool."

Direct injection is typically associated with diesel engines, though for gasoline applications it retains the use of spark plugs rather than using the heat generated by ultra-high compression to ignite the fuel/air mixture within the cylinder.

To apply direct injection to the small-block meant, among other things, swapping the former location of the intake and exhaust valves, redesigning the topography of the piston head, and devising a "tri-lobe" design for the camshaft.

To determine and then optimize such details, powertrain engineers used computational computer analysis to design, evaluate, and refine the combustion chamber before any tooling was produced. "We spent more than six-million hours of computational time just on the combustion system alone," Lee said.

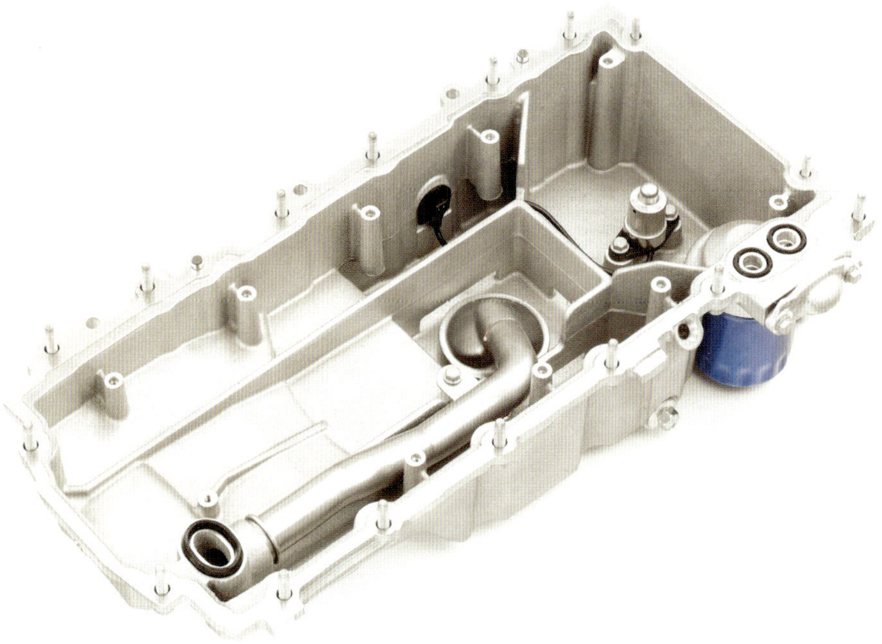

The dry sump oil pan is fed by a large tube to make sure engine parts are well lubricated even in the extreme g forces experienced on the race track.

Redesigning the valve train provided an opportunity to employ continuously variable valve timing, a technology that continually adjusts the opening and closing of the valves based on engine load. Such technology can achieve the seemingly opposite goals of improving both low-end torque and high-end horsepower, in part by installing a vane-type camshaft phaser on the front of the camshaft. The phaser adjusts the camshaft's angular orientation and optimizes the timing of the opening and closing of the valves based on driving conditions. To make sure the engine controller can respond with Corvette-like speed, data is drawn from four sources instead of the single segment used in many variable valve timing systems.

Such advanced variable valve timing technology also enables the introduction of a fuel-saving cylinder deactivation system to the Corvette, to operate that system in a range extended by 10 percent when compared to its use in vehicles powered by the previous-generation small-block, and to do so without any hesitation in returning to full power when the driver tips into the throttle.

"The Holy Grail for developing a performance car is delivering greater performance and more power with greater fuel economy, and that's what we've achieved," Juechter said when the new small-block was unveiled. "By leveraging technology, we are able to get more out of every drop of gasoline, and because of that we expect the new Corvette will be the most fuel-efficient 450 hp car on the market."

"Our objective for the development of the all-new LT1 [the engine's official name for use in the Stingray] was to raise the bar for performance car engines," added Mary Barra, GM's senior vice president for global product development. "We feel we have achieved that by delivering a true technological masterpiece that seamlessly integrates a suite of advanced technologies that can only be found on a handful of engines in the world.

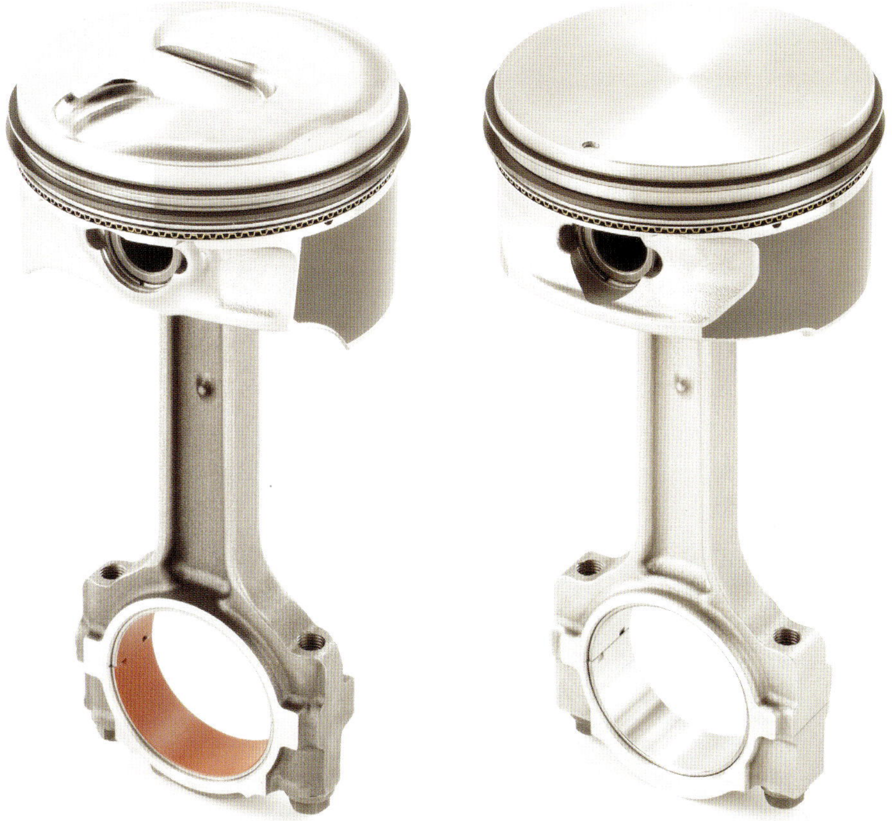

This image shows the new LT1 (left) and former LS3 (right) pistons, connecting rods, and connecting rod bearings.

This closeup shows some of the details of the sculpting of the top of the new Gen-5 small-block pistons. The sculpting was done to take advantage of direct injection technology.

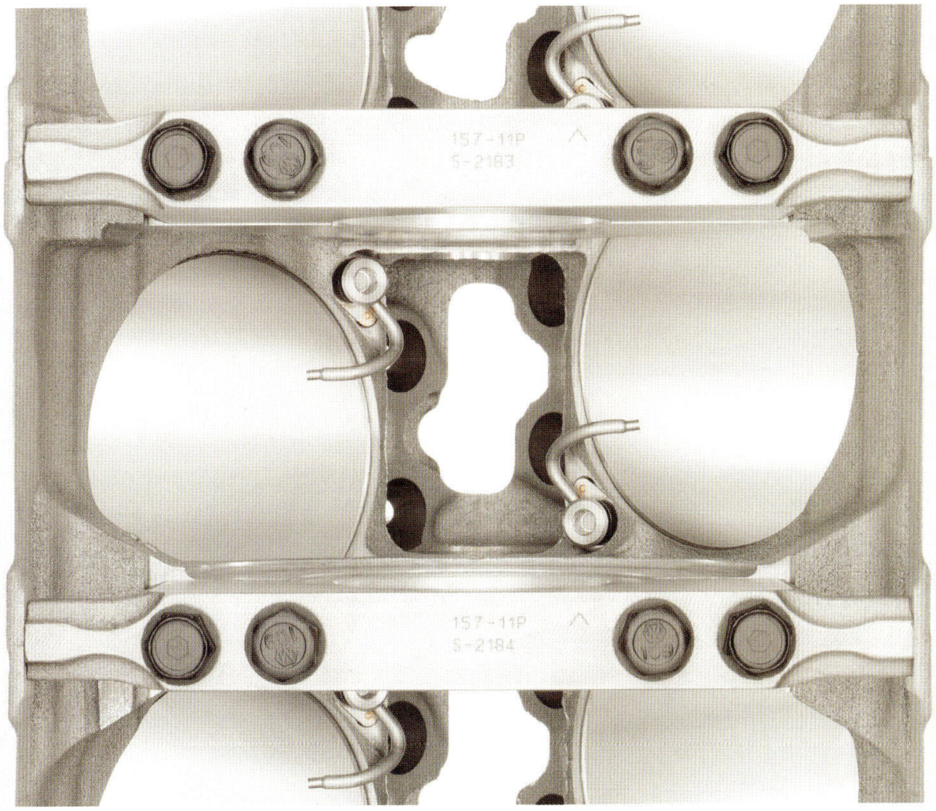

This closeup shows the valve ports, direct injection nozzle, and spark plug from the piston's perspective. cylinder head

This is the new Gen-5 small-block cam shaft with the cam phaser. The cam phaser enables continuously variable valve timing technology.

"What makes this engine truly special is the advanced combustion system that extracts the full potential of these technologies. The art and science behind that combustion system make the Corvette LT1 one of the most advanced V-8 engines in the world."

Cylinder deactivation—or Active Fuel Management as it is known within General Motors—turns the small-block V-8 into a very fuel-efficient V-4 in low-load driving situations, such as when simply cruising along a freeway.

To achieve cylinder deactivation, valve lifters are designed with inner and outer bodies that can be decoupled from normal operation as a single unit. When certain conditions exist, the outer body can be decoupled. For the new small-block, cylinder lifters are disabled on two alternate cylinders on each bank of the V-8. Fuel is also cut off to those cylinders. Oil circulation and pressure, however, remain at full force. The engine's electronic throttle control also is able to increase manifold pressure to maintain torque load and to assure instantaneous response when the deactivated cylinders are called on to return to full power production.

Because a four-cylinder engine runs inherently less smoothly than a V-8, new engine, transmission and exhaust system mounts were designed to isolate vibrations that might occur during cylinder deactivation. The use of the new mounts also helps extend the range in which the engine can operate on four cylinders.

The high-pressure fuel pump needed for direct injection is itself a source of noise, in part because of a "ticking" sound caused by a solenoid within the pump. Such pumps are typically mounted atop a cylinder head. But while developing the Gen-5 small-block, GM Powertrain engineers discovered they could reduce the solenoid "tick" with what they call "soft stop control strategy" software. They also decided to place the pump not atop a cylinder head but in the valley of the "V" and thus beneath the intake manifold. This not only blocks noise, but provides a packaging solution that helps maintain the engine's compact dimensions and the Corvette's low hood profile.

In addition to six million hours of computational analysis on the combustion system, GM Powertrain engineers spend another four million hours in analysis, including computational fluid dynamics, testing everything from engine structure to thermal and aural control.

But while software can be used to design and to control, it is hardware that pumps out the power. For the Generation-5 small-block, that hardware starts with the construction of a single-cylinder engine run on a dynometer and is used to verify the computerized engineering analysis. "We start with the combustion system and build the engine around it," Lee said.

The new small-block is topped by domed rocker covers, beneath which a patent-pending Positive Crankcase Ventilation system operates to enhance oil economy and life while lowering emissions. The covers also house the direct-mount ignition coils and are designed to be three times more effective in oil/air separation than on previous engines.

A new air-induction humidity sensor optimizes engine performance and fuel economy across the spectrum of ambient air humidity percentages. Engineers also devised a "four-into-one" short-header exhaust manifold. Dual-mode exhaust and engine-sound management systems vary the exhaust note depending on whether the driver has selected Tour, Sport, Track, or Off modes.

"The Corvette LT1 represents the most significant redesign in the small-block's nearly 60-year history, building on its legacy to make one of the world's best engines even better," said Sam Winegarden, GM vice president for global powertrain engineering.

"More than just great horsepower, the LT1 has been optimized to produce a broader power band. Below 4,000 rpm, the torque of the Corvette LT1 is comparable to that of the legendary 7.0L LS7 out of the current Corvette Z06. The LT1 is a sweetheart of a power plant, and drivers will feel its tremendous torque and power at every notch on the tachometer."

THE RUNNING OF THE MULES

Once the combustion system is validated and efficiencies analyzed, prototype V-8 engines—or "mules" in engineer speak—are created for testing both in the lab and on the road. Next comes what engineers call the "beta" engine—powerplants built to production specifications but constructed of rapid-prototyping tools and techniques.

"Power and torque came relatively easy, and so did fuel economy," Lee said. "But people don't really understand how hard it is to design a lubrication system in a car that's race-track capable."

As it has been from the beginning, the small-block continues to use proven pushrod valve activation.

Similar to the development of the Stingray's chassis and aerodynamics, powertrain engineers worked closely with the Corvette racing team in the planning and development of the Generation-5 small-block.

Lee said that to simulate in the engine lab what happens when a Corvette goes around a 1.2g turn on a banked race track, a special stand had to be created to tip the engine as much as 50 degrees from level.

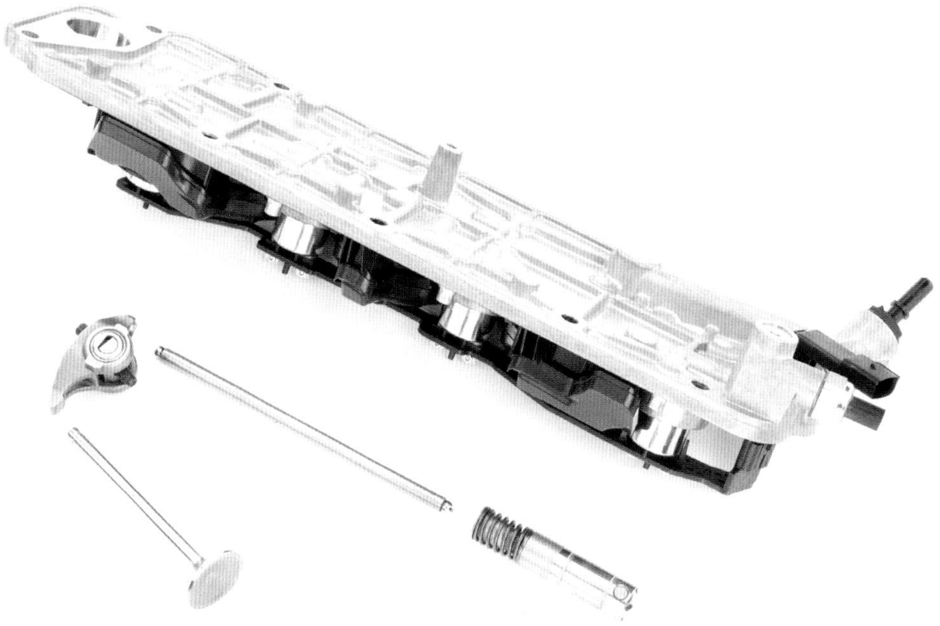

This is the hardware that makes continuously variable valve timing function properly.

"The oil pump cannot suck air," Lee said. For the Stingray, the Generation-5 small-block gets a unique and variable displacement oil pump.

"To have that capability is extremely challenging," he said, adding that such extreme forces don't come into play when developing V-8 engines for pickup trucks, "not even for the Camaro."

To keep the Corvette small-block light but strong, the block and heads are made from aluminum alloy. To help keep the engine cool, pressure-actuated oil jets spray the underside of each piston as well as the surrounding cylinder wall to enhance performance at start-up and at high engine speeds. The engine also can be equipped with dry-sump lubrication technology designed for high-stress driving, such as on a race track.

The block features a deep-skirt design and structural oil pan to enhance strength and reduce vibration. Bulkheads stiffen the engine structure and enable six-bolt, cross-bolted main-bearing caps that limit crankshaft flex. Nodular iron

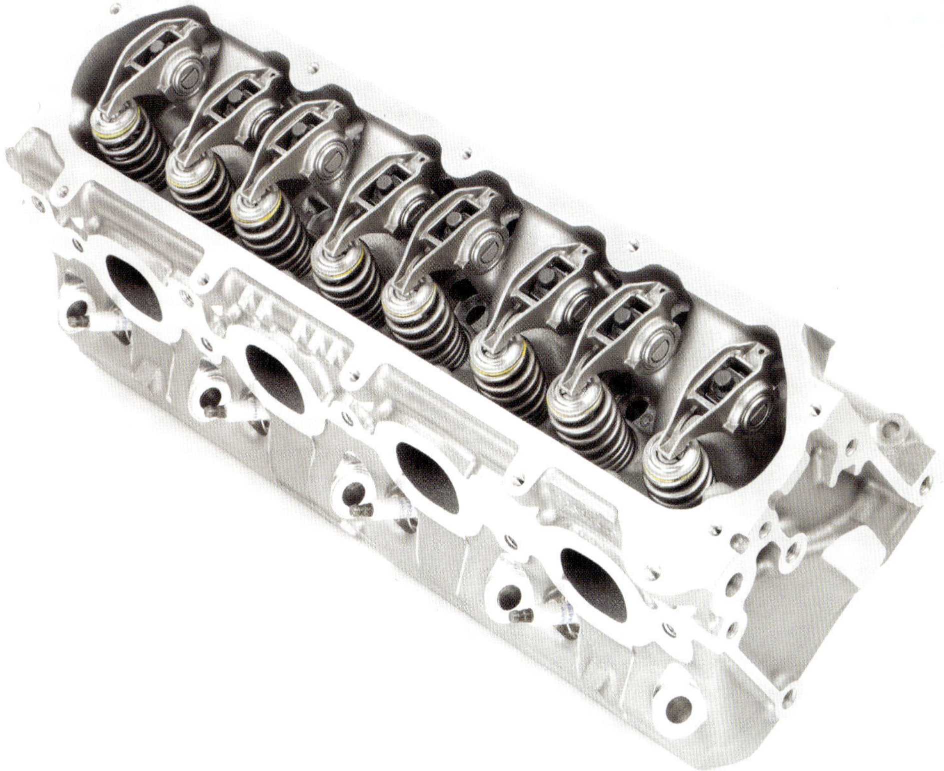

This photo shows the hardware that operates the active fuel management technology that can turn the V-8 into a V-4 for enhanced fuel economy in low-load situations such as cruising along an Interstate highway.

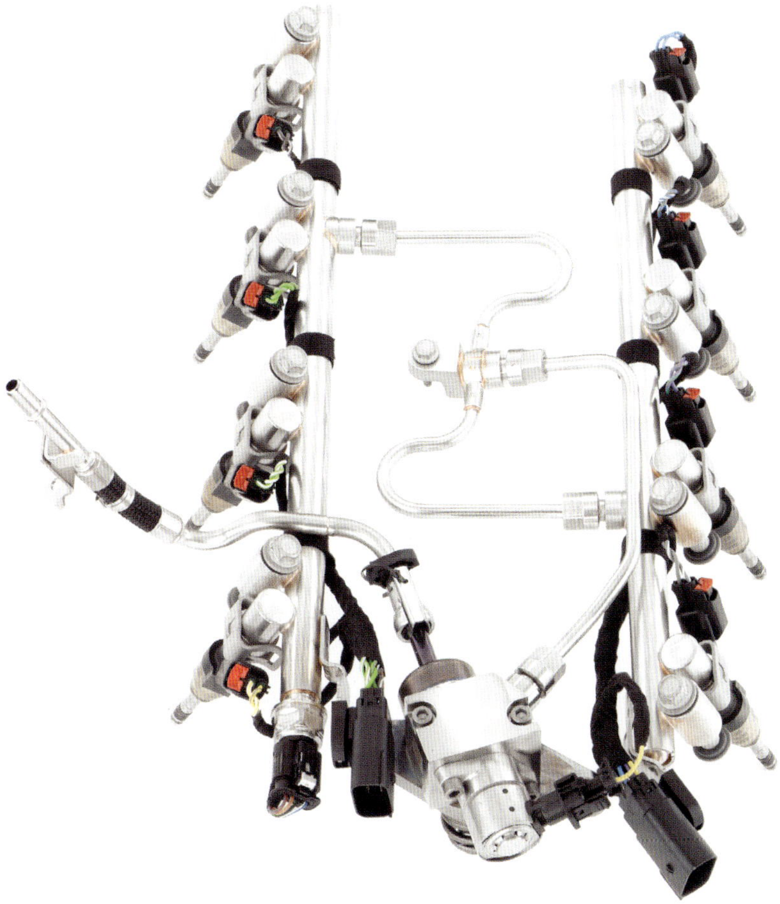

This is the hardware for the direct injection system on the new Gen-5 small-block V-8.

main-bearing caps, used instead of the typical powdered-metal caps, are stronger and reduce harmonic vibration.

Once such engines are performing properly—in everything from power delivery to fuel efficiency, and from noise control to durability—production tooling is created and installed at the Tonawanda engine production facility, located on 190 acres near the banks of the Niagara River in Buffalo, New York.

PUTTING IT ALL TOGETHER

Production at the original Tonawanda plant dates to 1938. Ground was broken the previous year for what at first was called the Chevrolet Motor and Axle Plant, which has produced more than 70 million engines for various GM vehicles as well as building aircraft engines during World War II and for the Korean conflict. A $400-million investment began in 2010 to get the plant tooled up for production of the new small-block, with an even larger investment to build the next-generation Ecotech 2.0- and 2.5-liter four-cylinder engines at the same 3.1-million square-foot facility. GM also builds small-block V-8s in Mexico and Canada, but all the LT1 engines for the new Corvette will come from the historic Tonawanda facility. Tonawanda also builds V-8 engines for Chevrolet and GMC trucks, and four-cylinder engines for the Chevrolet Malibu and Cadillac ATS.

"Tonawanda is to manufacturing like the small-block is to us at Powertrain," Lee said. "It was designed by architect Albert Kahn, built aircraft engines for World War II, and holds the world record for the most engines produced in one day—8,832, produced by members of UAW Local 774 in a single day in 1988.

"GM didn't have money to invest in it in the late '90s and it became pretty run down. The decision to put the Gen-5 small-block in the plant was a resurrection for the plant, and it's become a Phoenix rising from the ashes.

"It was gutted—even the floor was removed and new concrete poured. There's all new equipment and it's bright and shiny and new."

"There are block machine modules with gantries with robots going back and forth, it's like a ballet," Lee said. "But, he added, "the assembly line is not fully robotized. People are putting engines together. People are still the best device for assembling something this complicated."

Those "people" will include those buying the new Stingray: Chevrolet has offered an Engine Build Experience program for C6 Corvette buyers and plans to establish a similar program for C7 customers who want to travel to the National Corvette Museum, which is across the road from the Corvette assembly plant in Bowling Green, Kentucky.

Perhaps as soon as the fall of 2014, those C7 buyers also may be able to drive their Stingrays just across the highway from the museum and assembly plant and do some laps on the National Corvette Museum Motorsports Park. Groundbreaking was scheduled for the summer of 2013, with the facility to open Labor Day weekend in 2014.

Before any customers were to do any driving, however, the new seventh-generation Corvette and its new fifth-generation small-block engine—as well as all of the car's other components and systems—would have to be tested on the roads and around a variety of race tracks by Tadge Juechter and his engineering team.

This photo shows the direct injection hardware in place in the valley of the LT1 engine.

CHAPTER

7

ON THE ROAD, BUT UNDER

You could say that Josh Holder was the keeper of the keys—the keys to the 2014 Corvette Stingray, that is.

Josh Holder's responsibilities as engineering launch manager for the C7 Chevrolet Corvette included making sure prototypes were built and tested (including crash-tested to validate their safety), that all components and systems were properly integrated, and then moving from Michigan to Kentucky to help make sure the assembly process rolled out smoothly.

Or at least you could say that Josh Holder was the keeper of the keys to the C7 Corvette Stingray in the months when it was progressing from a designer's dream, engineer's challenge, and assembly plant production project into the car sitting on a dealer's showroom floor, awaiting the handing of the keys to the sports car's new owner.

Holder, a western Montana native and a graduate first of Weber State in Utah and then Purdue in Indiana, was well into the second decade of his engineering career at General Motors. He had spent most of that time on the Corvette team.

For the C7, Holder was engineering launch manager, which means he managed the building and testing of prototype vehicles and the integration of all their various systems. Holder worked so closely with the assembly plant at Bowling Green on the start of the car's production and launch that he temporarily moved from southeastern Michigan to western Kentucky.

"We have functional experts in structure, chassis, powertrain, and more," Holder explained. "My job is to integrate those functions so we have not just good subsystems but a good car. My primary purpose is to get this car launched."

CAMOUFLAGE

A camouflaged prototype, or IVER (Integration Vehicle Engineering Release), works its way around the Michelin tire company's test track in South Carolina.

HIDING THE STINGRAY

What Corvette owners see is their car, sitting there all shiny and ready to drive. What they don't see are all the versions of that car that had to be built, tested, validated—even crashed—to make sure their Stingray is not only fun and fast, but also dependable and durable, fuel-efficient and safe.

In late 2010, fifteen "mule" vehicles (the first iteration of the car that would eventually become the C7 Corvette) were built in a prototype workshop near the GM Tech Center in Warren, Michigan. They were engineered around prototype chassis built to C7 specifications, but with what Holder called "scabbed over" parts from the C5 Corvette. "The new exterior and interior weren't even finished at that point," Holder said.

Some of the mules were used for architectural development to ensure that the new all-aluminum chassis structure would work as designed. Some of the mules were used to verify the car's crashworthiness—which means they existed only to be violently destroyed—and to provide data proving that the new structure properly protected its occupants in a worst-case situation. Other mules were used in nondestructive body and chassis development. Yet others were used for powertrain integration development with the new, fifth-generation small-block V-8 and the new Corvette transmissions.

Sometimes the powertrain integration mules needed to venture outside General Motors' proving grounds and onto public roads, so they were disguised to look like C6 Corvette Grand Sports—though if someone looked closely at the interior, they might have noticed that the instrument clusters were borrowed from the Chevrolet Camaro.

Such cobbling is typical of mule vehicles. Because many of the production-intent components were still in development, the C7 mules were equipped with two separate body-control modules: one tied to the new chassis and powertrain hardware, and another to operate the components borrowed from older cars, such as the power windows.

IVER TIME

Like their hoofed counterparts, mule vehicles aren't all that pretty; they are workhorses designed for specific (if limited) purposes. Starting in September 2011 and continuing into early 2012, the mules were replaced by the IVER, which is short for Integration Vehicle Engineering Release.

Components on the IVERs are prototypes of the production-intent parts destined for the Bowling Green assembly line. And to make sure those components can be properly assembled at the plant, key staffers from Bowling Green, including members of the United Auto Workers, traveled regularly to Michigan to work with GM engineers and technicians on the IVERs.

"We had people who were hourly employees who will be the leaders for their areas come up to work with us," Holder said. "Build issues were found very early."

By bringing personnel from Bowling Green into the IVER construction process,

Technicians and engineers based at the GM Tech Center in Warren, Michigan, and people who work on the Corvette assembly line at Bowling Green, Kentucky, work together as various proposed components are checked for precise fitment on one of the first C7 IVER prototypes.

potential assembly line issues that might not otherwise have been noticed until cars were working their way along the assembly line can be dealt with as hiccups rather than emergencies. For example, a UAW member might notice that there's simply not enough clearance to install a part, and either the part or a tool or some other part of the process can be adjusted long before the line is moving at the Bowling Green factory.

Eighty-five C7 Corvette IVERs were built and assigned to Corvette engineering groups for various purposes: crash testing; powertrain controls calibration; chassis controls calibration; ride and handling development; noise and vibration development; body sealing development; HVAC (heating, ventilation and air conditioning) and thermal development; electrical function and software development; durability testing; data acquisition (for subsystem and component laboratory testing); and the so-called golden cars, vehicles designated as "shared usage" to be taken on "ride trip" evaluations.

Issues will arise in any vehicle development program, especially one involving as much new componentry and innovative technology as the seventh-generation Corvette.

"One of the tremendous challenges with this car has been active fuel management," Holder said. "It's very complicated [on any vehicle, but especially on a car] with high expectations for the driving dynamics."

One challenge is overcoming the vibration involved when half of an engine's cylinders are deactivated. But, Holder said, the engine calibration work was successful. "Ninety-nine percent of customers won't even know it [AFM] is there," Holder said.

A plastic model of the proposed exhaust pipe is checked to make sure there is enough clearance during the "marriage" ceremony as a prototype body and powertrain are joined together during the early IVER-building process.

Here's a view from beneath the car of the marriage between the body and the drivetrain. Note the white (prototype) exhaust pipes and mufflers.

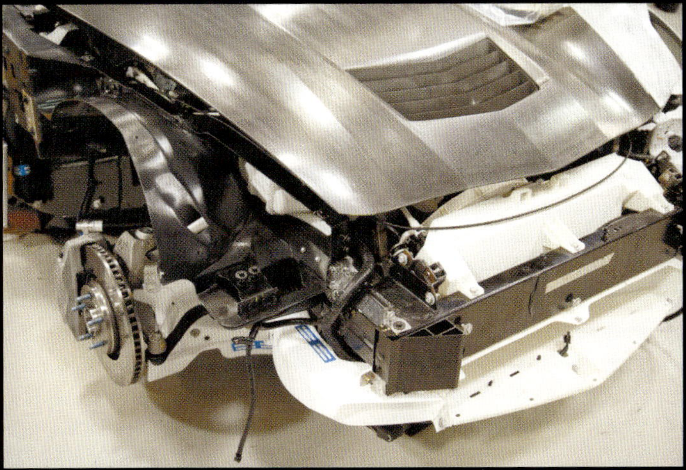

Early in the process of building IVER cars, various component design engineers brought their prototypes parts—the various white parts in the photographs—so they could be verified as properly fitting and also provided necessary clearances for the assembly process. This prototype is now on display at the National Corvette Museum.

Throughout the prototype-building process, laser measuring devices are used to assure proper fitment based on designs from both the styling and engineering departments. Here, Jeffrey Dingee of GM technical staff wields the device.

As an IVER body is constructed, components such as the magnesium steering wheel mount and other dashboard components are secured into place.

"A close second was electronics," he said, adding that what was once a 99 percent hardware issue has become a "software activity" involving the integration of myriad complex components. For example, one electronic control module may need permission from another module to trigger a function, but that may not happen until queries have been sent to other modules to make sure an action does not run at cross-purposes with other vehicle or subsystem operations. It can be a redundant and energy-sapping process within the car's computer and electrical systems. But everything was sorted out, and Holder was pleased to report in December 2012 that "we have not had to flatbed a car off a ride yet."

Holder made his flatbed comment just before several of the "golden" IVERs set out on what was basically the final sign-off road trip for the IVER stage of development. That trip took the cars from Michigan to Bowling Green and on into the mountainous areas of Tennessee and North Carolina and back again.

So far, so good.

A couple of months later, the dreaded flatbed was needed, but not because of a glitch in electronic component integration. Instead, a truck had to be called out when a C7 prototype crashed during testing on a remote stretch of roadway in Arizona, where the car ricocheted off a guardrail into the rocky face of a mountain.

The C7 Corvette IVERs were built in two batches. The second batch (IVER 2.0, if you will) was built on what was discovered during testing of the first batch. The next step in the development process was building 20

However, components such as the steering wheel mount and other brackets are soon hidden beneath the dashboard and the steering column and its assorted switchgear.

PPV—product and process verification —vehicles, which were built right on the assembly line at Bowling Green, just before the end of 2012.

"The first car—and remember, these are hugely complex machines—was built on the line with very little stoppage," Holder said, adding that this was accomplished on an assembly line that was still building the C6 Corvette. Building two vehicles on the same line (especially such different vehicles) makes the process much more complex.

Holder remembered when the first C6 Corvette was making its way down the Bowling Green line: "The trunk of the first C6 was full of parts" that were not installed on the line, he admitted, "and we pushed it off the line." That first car wasn't even running under its own power.

But that wasn't the case for the first C7 PPV.

"The plant manager gets into the car, pushes the button. It starts, and he drives it off the line—under tremendous applause."

This image of an IVER under construction shows some of the structure adjacent to the passenger's seat.

Hourly employees from Bowling Green work with technicians and engineers in Michigan during the prototype-building process. Their presence helps with the transition from styling and engineering design to the actual assembly of those components into a finished automobile. It's one thing to build nearly one-off prototypes, but another to do production on a moving assembly line. It's better to identify any potential issues a year or more in advance when there's time to devise a solution without slowing production.

Because Bowling Green was busy building C6 Corvettes while the C7 was being developed, the body shop for the C7 was constructed and put into operation in a rented warehouse in Michigan where frames and chassis for the prototype Stringrays were fabricated. After the last of the C6 cars and the last of the C7 IVER prototypes were completed, the body shop equipment was moved to and installed at the Bowling Green assembly plant.

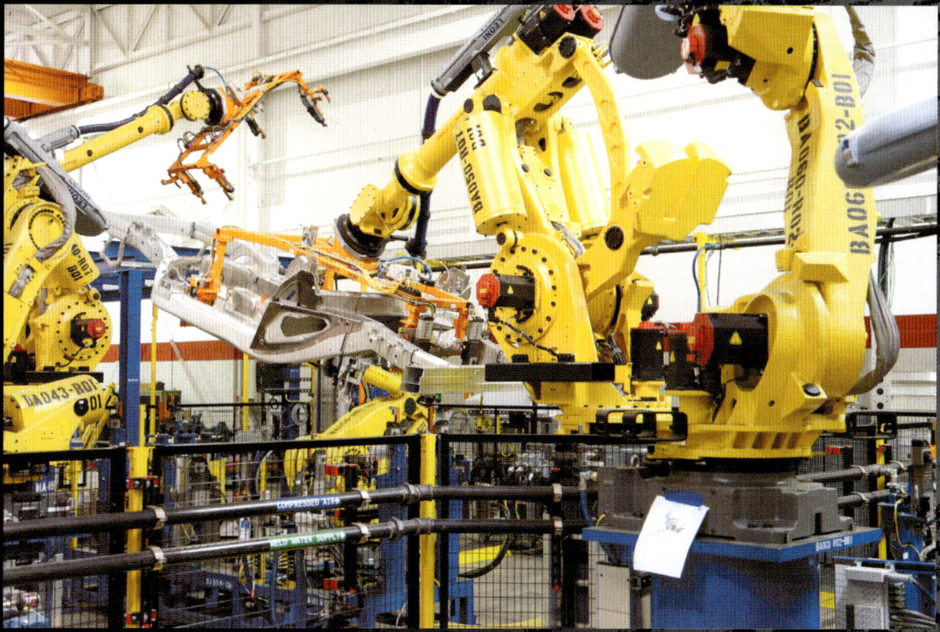

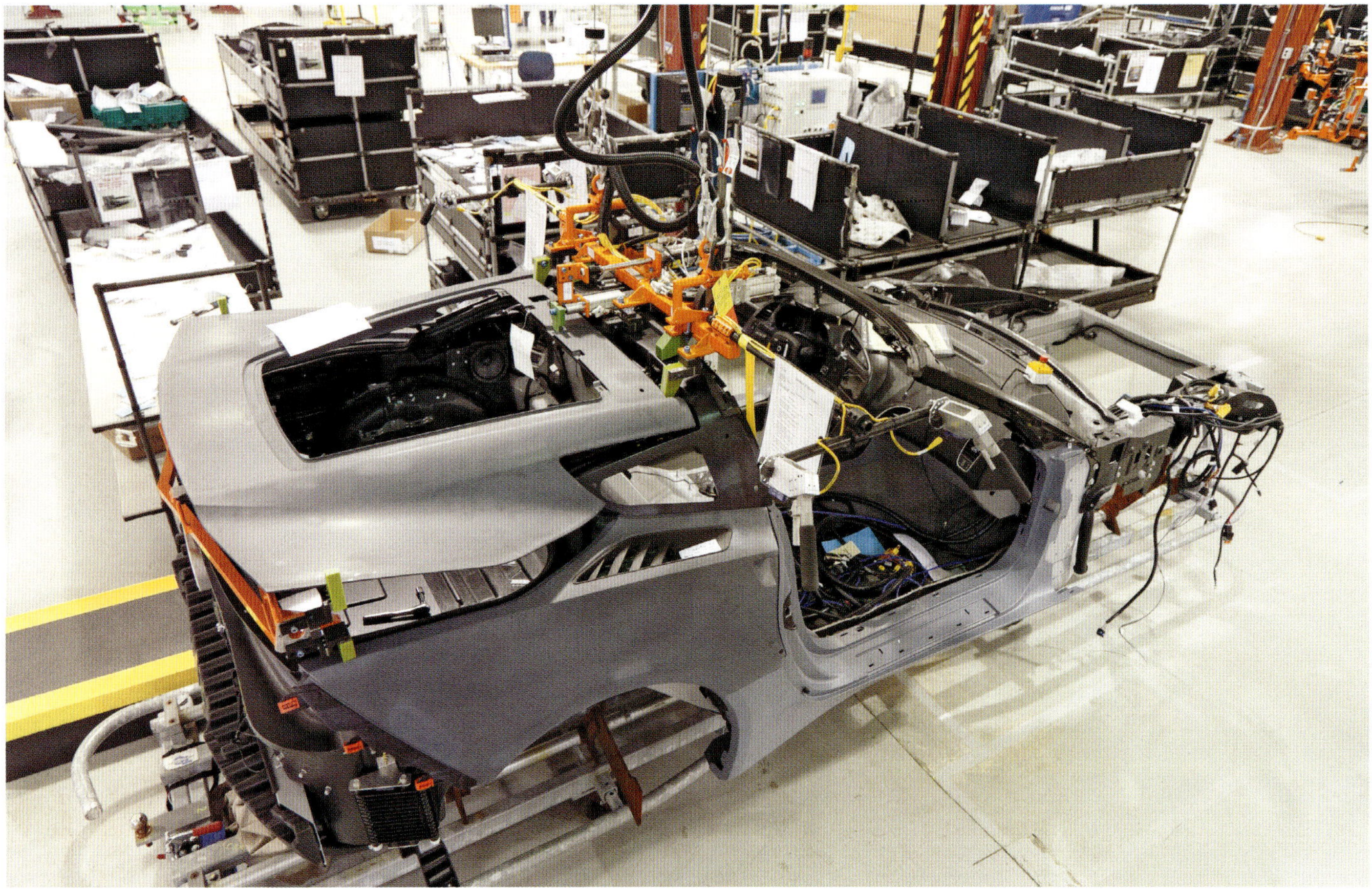

A C7 IVER is just about ready for its engine and drivetrain to be installed.

A prototype C7 Corvette body awaits mating to its powertrain.

One of the new Gen-5 small-block V-8 engines awaits installation in a C7 Corvette prototype.

ONE GENERATION SAYS GOODBYE, ANOTHER SAYS HELLO

While those 20 PPV cars were being tested, the last of the C6 cars was assembled and the assembly line was reconfigured for production of the C7. Starting in early 2013, Manufacturing Validation Build C7s rolled off the Bowling Green line. As their name indicates, these cars were built to validate the manufacturing processes. The first 50 were deemed "non-salable" units, destined for testing and then destruction. The next 300 would be "salable" units, cars that comprise what is known at General Motors as the "captive test fleet." Such cars are assigned to specific GM staffers for daily driving and final evaluation on public roads and are later sold as used cars.

Once all aspects of the vehicles had been validated, production of new C7 Corvettes for Chevrolet dealer showrooms started in the summer of 2013.

Among those with whom Holder eagerly shared keys to the various C7 prototype vehicles was Jim Mero, whose job likely would win the "what's the best occupation in the world?" contest among Corvette enthusiasts. Why?

Because Jim Mero is the vehicle dynamics ride-and-handling engineer for the C7 Corvette.

"I do all the suspension tuning—springs, bars, shocks, tires, steering," Mero explained. "I do most of the high-speed stuff."

That high-speed stuff includes spending workday hours driving Corvette prototypes (and sometimes actual production cars) to their limits on test and racing tracks. It was Mero who was behind the wheel when the ZR1 version of the C6 Corvette turned a lap of the famed Nurburgring circuit in Germany in less than seven minutes, 20 seconds—a production record at the time.

Mero does most of the high-speed development driving for the new Corvette, and Alex McDonald takes the wheel when that testing involves the tuning of the electronic control systems for the anti-lock brakes, traction control, and related systems.

Like McDonald, Mero is an accomplished racing driver. "I raced for 20 years," Mero said. "Open-wheel—Formula Ford and Formula Vee—showroom stock and late model." Mero won sports car racing track championships and raced in the national Runoffs in 1994 and 1995, but then switched to stock cars on short-track ovals. Mero even raced in the famed 24 Hours of Le Mans, but said he found short-track stock car racing to be the "hardest racing I've ever done."

"I was a typical road racer, thinking there are only two turns and they're basically the same," he said. "But they cleaned my clock for two years. You're a tenth of a second off the pole and you're gridded twentieth!"

Mero raced until 2006. "It was my best year in late models when I had to hang it up," he said, "due to the demands of the job and simply getting older. It was tough to step away from competition because I finally had a few wins and was fourth in points. But racing is a second full-time job, and pushing 50 years old I was losing the interest and energy needed to keep the racing operation going. I loved the driving, but dreaded the week nights working on the car until midnight to have it ready for the next week."

A rear hatch awaits installation.

With their engines nearby, IVERS are in their stalls, awaiting component installation

Hood up, this prototype awaits its exhaust system to be installed next.

Tail pipes, at least as they appeared at the IVER stage of C7 development.

Mero went to work for General Motors after graduating with a degree in mechanical engineering from Lawrence Tech. He started in structural analysis, then in occupant protection and vehicle crash-testing before working on interior engineering. He finally got behind the wheel doing chassis tuning in the 1980s, just in time to be part of the driving team doing the 24-hour test regimen with the C4 Corvette.

Mero's involvement with the C7 Corvette began long before there were any prototypes to drive.

"We started when the car was in the advanced [planning] phase," Mero said, explaining that "we" was Mero and Jeff Mosher, an engineer and racing driver who also is "our math analysis guy, and he's spectacular," Mero explained. "He's a math guy who races cars as well. He understands the dynamics of the car, and how to create the computerized mathematical models that simulate the dynamics the Corvette, optimizing performance the Corvette team—and Corvette customers—want from their cars. Occasionally I'm at a loss of words to explain some dynamic phenomenon, and as a race car driver, Jeff knows how to extract the information from me."

"We didn't have a clean sheet of paper," Mero said. "But we had the ability to influence every part on the car. Everything. From the road wheel to the steering wheel. We completely optimized everything we could."

One—well, actually four—of the things Mero and Mosher needed to optimize were the tires for all C7 Stingrays rolling out of the Bowling Green assembly plant. Goodyear was the traditional supplier for Corvette. Michelin, however, earned a place in the OE (original equipment) race after its success with the Corvette Racing team and then on the highest-performance C6 variants available from Chevrolet dealerships.

Building IVER vehicles involves more than wrenches and adhesives. Computers are used for various reasons, from verifying the latest hardware changes to flashing updated codes to the various on-board computers. Computers also are used to download data after the cars go through their various dynamic test cycles.

Operation of the power top and its trunk lid are tested on a C7 Corvette convertible prototype.

The Corvette engineering team knew the best way to get the best tire on the new Stingray was to have a shootout between Goodyear and Michelin. In the fall of 2010, both tire makers provided tires built to the specifications of the new Stingray that were narrower than those of the Grand Sport and Z06—245 millimeters wide instead of 275 in front, and 285 millimeters instead of 325 at the rear—for reduced drag.

Despite the specifications, Mero was concerned about whether such tires could provide the desired grip for extreme cornering maneuvers, so he decided to use a C6 Z06 as the track car for the shootout. The race was staged in utmost secrecy at Virginia International Raceway. If the tires could handle the cornering capabilities of a 505-horsepower C6 Z06, he knew they would be suitable for the C7 Z51.

For the test, the C6 Z06 was fitted with prototype wheels designed to carry the new tires and to fit over the Z06 brakes. "In my first session on both Goodyears and Michelins, my lap times were more than a second faster than my baseline runs on the Goodyear Gen-2 Z06 production tires," Mero was delighted to report. "We ran 16 extensive tests on the tires from Goodyear and Michelin to determine the best tire for the C7."

Michelin won, and it's Michelin tires which will, in Mero's words, "define" the C7 Corvette.

"I'm really happy with the fact we were able to do a shootout," Mero said. "We knew we were getting the best tire for the car, and while running the shootout, I was astonished at how good the car was going to be. As a performance guy, I had been fighting for bigger tires, but Michelin hit it out of the park."

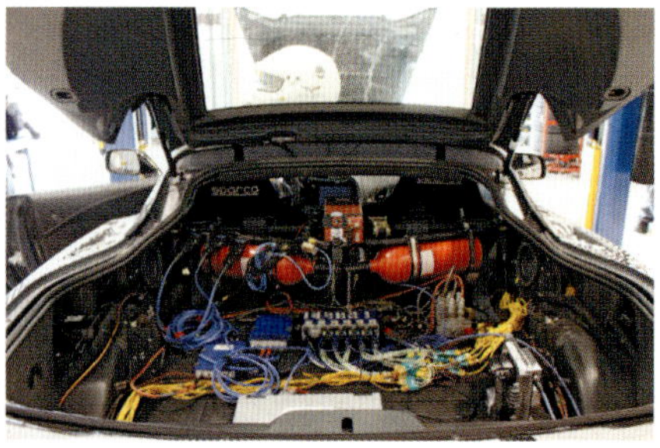

Your Corvette might carry golf clubs in its trunk. The prototypes used to develop your car carried all sorts of data recording equipment, and even fire-suppressant gear when doing high-speed runs on race tracks.

The C7 Corvette's chief engineer Tadge Juechter makes sure Ken Parkinson (left), executive director of design for Chevrolet and GMC, and John Spencer (center), C7 launch manager at Bowling Green, understand the Stingray engineers' vision so components will be designed and fitted precisely.

The pattern for the C7 camouflage was nicknamed "Cartoon Network" by the Stingray design and engineering teams.

The hood vent is surrounded by camouflage.

As if the swirling-patterned camouflage wasn't enough to hide the lines of the C7, matte-black covers were placed over the camouflage to hide the lines even more when the IVER prototypes were heading out onto public roads for dynamic testing.

Mero and Mosher returned to VIR for their first on-track experience with a C7 mule equipped with the new LT1 small-block V-8 and the new Michelin tires. "We went to VIR with a mule car to shake it down and see what it was going to be like," Mero said.

And what was it like?

"All the analytical stuff that Jeff did really paid off," he said. "Right out of the box it was better than the C6, which is still one of the best cars out there."

Mero later worked extensively with IVER-level prototypes, dialing in such things as ride frequencies, spring weights, suspension bushings, shock absorber turning, weight distribution nuances, etc.

Early in 2012, Mero and Mosher traveled to South Carolina to Michelin's Laurens Proving Grounds, for the first tuning session on an IVER car and the first round of Michelin tires. Not only was the test important, but it also was revealing, and on multiple levels, Mero said.

One level of reveal came because "you can't run a race track with vinyl [camouflage] on the car, so you just run tape [to keep some styling details out of sight]." Mero said it took approval from on high, and only slightly short of an act of God, to approve the removal of the C7's camo covering, but it had to be done. "That's when we got our first glimpse of what this new car was going to look like," Mero said.

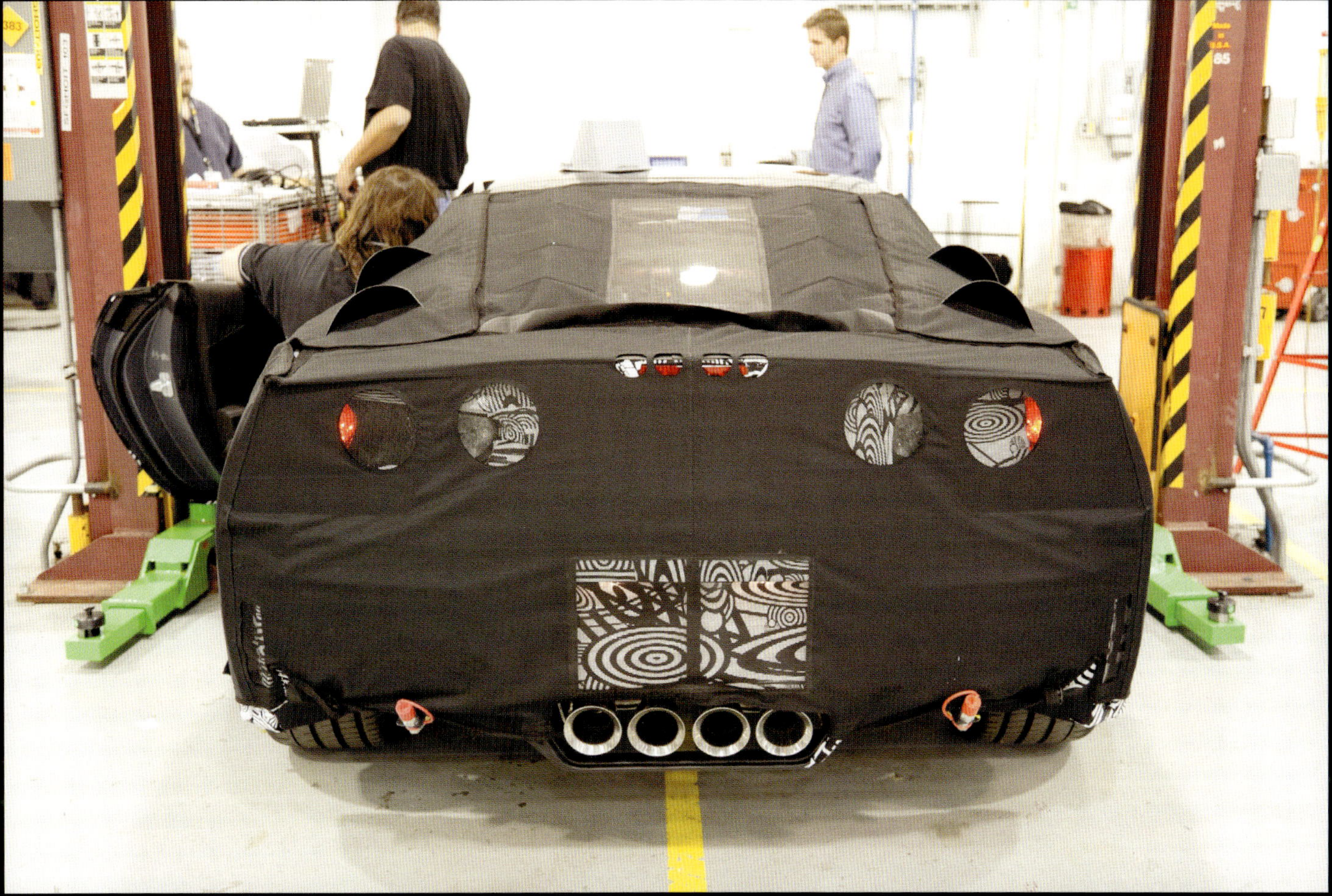

A group of finished prototypes await their dynamic duties. For some, it may involve high-speed testing. For others, their destiny is to be sacrificed in crash testing.

But even more important to Mero than appearance is performance, especially at the extreme "edge" of the car's capability.

"I was blown away," Mero said. "We thought we were hitting home runs with the PS2 [Michelin Pilot Sport PS2] and PS Cup [Pilot Sport Cup] tires on the [C6] ZR1. I was surprised how much grip these new tires had. They were a big step down in size, but the technology made the car faster and easier to drive. "You could have the best suspension in the world, but if you don't have good tires..." Mero mused, "tires define the car."

And that was only the first round of Michelins.

"Jeff Mosher put together a twenty-five page debriefing of data for Michelin to know where to go for the next round of tires," Mero said, who throughout the summer was doing evaluation drives, pushing each successive generation of the tires produced by a Michelin team led by engineers Lee Willard and John Church to their or the car's dynamic limits.

"The tires were in evolution until October, when we had our final submission," Mero said. "The evolution of the car throughout the summer and into the fall was pretty involved," he added, "but every time we stepped away from one phase [of the development], the car was not only really fast but it drove better."

Early on, Mero was surprised by some of the "lateral load transfer" he was feeling "This car was a little more biased to the rear than the current [C6] car," he said, explaining that it took two weeks to discover the rear suspension needed a significant increase in rear roll stiffness.

"On the track, when I loosen a car up, I prefer to do it in small steps because the down side of going too far is backing it into the fence," Mero explained. "We were making small steps to move the TLLTD (tire lateral load transfer distribution) to the rear."

After examining the data, however, Mosher realized a bigger step was needed. "Once again, Mosher's the one who figured it out," Mero said.

Even after such seemingly significant breakthroughs are made, however, testing isn't finished. Mero said there always are slight differences between the (hand-built) IVERS and (assembly-plant produced) PPVs that have to be sorted, some "messaging" to the magnetic suspension system, steering, and eLSD. After that, confirmation of the package on the convertible version of the C7, and almost immediately, work starts on the 2015 model year Corvette.

Tuning a car such as the Corvette is made even more challenging because there are multiple suspension setups. You can get the car in its regular guise with standard Bilstein shocks. Then there's the higher-performance Z51 suspension with even more aggressive Michelin tires and larger Bilstein shocks, or with the advanced Magnetic Ride Control technology.

Much of Mero's driving is done at General Motors' Milford Proving Grounds in Michigan, and especially on the MRC—the Milford Road Course, a hilly, demanding circuit designed to push performance cars to their limits.

A trio of C7 Stingray prototypes and a pair of C6 Corvettes are ready for cold-weather testing at a General Motors facility in Michigan's Upper Peninsula.

The heavily disguised C7 prototypes head out onto the snow-covered test track. Automotive engineers like to test vehicles in temperature extremes ranging from at least plus to minus 40-degrees Celsius, or from 104 above to 40 below on the Fahrenheit scale.

The MRC was designed as sort of a mini-Nurburgring and built under the direction of former GM car czar Bob Lutz, and is nicknamed the "Lutzring." The track was designed by Mero, former Corvette engineer Mike Neal, and analysis engineer Joe Ryan.

"I think Bob Lutz liked the track because he was always buzzing us in his fighter jet when we were testing there," Mero said.

"The MRC is really a good track," Mero said, "but all the turns but one are mechanical-grip turns, not aero [high-speed] turns, and this car has way more downforce so we needed to go to tracks that had aero turns.

"You don't want to tune a car to just one track," he added. "We chose VIR and Road Atlanta, as well as Michelin's track at Laurens, which has both aero and mechanical turns."

Mero was interviewed for this book early in 2013. He had been doing "shock work and steering tuning" in mountain passes in the southern California desert and in the mountains east of Phoenix, had been on several race tracks, and was just about to make yet another visit to VIR to do a final sign-off on the electric power steering calibration.

His next project would be the 24-hour test.

"That's a big deal," Mero said.

The test is a twist on a 24-hour race, but is staged in segments until the car, driven to its limit by Mero and other top drivers, has completed a cumulative 24 hours without any issues. The clock starts when the car leaves the pits with a full tank of fuel and stops when the car begins its cool-down laps.

The fuel tank can be refilled. Worn tires can be changed. Brake pads as well. But no other wear issues are tolerated, nor are any sort of parts failures. Should such a thing occur, the issues are addressed and the 24-hour clock starts all over again.

In addition to on-road testing in various ambient weather conditions—from the cold of Canada to the heat of Death Valley—the C7 undergoes a series of tests inside the climate chamber at GM's Milford Proving Grounds in Michigan (top), then makes its way to the GM Tech Center in Warren (inset, bottom).

"So every second of the 24 hours, the car is running hot," Mero said.

"That's a hell of a durability test for any car," said Corvette engineering launch manager Josh Holder. "And it's done in addition to all other GM test experiences."

But for the C7 Corvette, the 24-hour test is just a preliminary event. Sometime during the summer of 2013, Mero and his car will go to Germany for testing on the hallowed ground of Nordschliefe, the historic and nearly 13-mile long, 73-turn north circuit at the Nurburgring.

For high-speed tire testing, the canvas cover is removed from the C7 prototype.

A pair of Corvette prototypes are prepped for on-track testing.

"Everything about this car [the C7] has exceeded my expectations," Mero said, adding that he was absolutely flabbergasted by the electronic power steering system.

"In this market, steering is everything," he said. "Initially I was against EPS. During the inception of the C7, we were evaluating EPS on other vehicles. Although suitable for those cars, I didn't think in three years EPS would be ready for prime time on a supercar. Boy, was I wrong. ZF's technical capability and steering engineer/manager Scott Montgomery's expertise proved that EPS was the best choice."

"Then we started tuning the steering on the track with the new Michelin tires, a 50/50 weight distribution, we were looking at lap times we were hoping would be one or two seconds better than the old Z51 actually bettering it by four to five seconds, and suddenly the [C6] Grand Sport was slower by over a second. The steering and the entire package wildly exceeded my expectations."

Mero's were not the only expectations the new C7 Corvette had to meet—or, hopefully, exceed. While he was testing the car near the limits of its adhesion, other members of the Corvette engineering team were in mules, IVERs, and preproduction cars, testing and turning, integrating and validating various systems with the goal of making the Stingray even better than the sum of its parts.

"It involves miles of driving on some pretty punishing roads around the proving grounds to accelerate what our 99th-percentile customer would do over the life a car," said Holder. "We collect all kinds of data. Typically, the cars are heavily instrumented so we can take that data back to subsystem and component testing in the lab and duplicate that duty cycle on production-tooled parts."

In addition to the IVER vehicles, "we had double that number of bucks," Holder said, explaining that those bucks could be fully-trimmed bodies, half cars, a rear-suspension module, or a complete interior buck, all used for specific testing procedures." All that learning feeds into the later builds," he said.

"One thing Corvette customers would find surprising and interesting is some of the tests we put these cars through," Holder said. "While track testing is exciting, it's expected. What they may not expect is some of the abuse testing we put these cars through that most customers would cringe at.

"For example, the Belgian Block Road is the worst cobblestone job you can imagine, but we drive hundreds of thousands of miles on it.

"We'll run a car through corrosion testing. Corrosion testing is a grit trough with a prescribed amount of dirt and mica and salt in solution six inches deep, and we plow the car through time and time again. And we take full vehicles and stick them inside a corrosion chamber—basically a sauna ninety or so degrees inside a salt steam bath—and it gets into places you'd never expect."

Holder said the salt steam bath simulates 50 years of being exposed to the salt air on the Florida coast.

Holder and his team also do specific testing on the Corvette convertible for such things as body sealing and wind noise, as well as abuse tests involving the

Jim Mero prepares to take a Stingray prototype out onto the Michelin test track in South Carolina to check out the latest iteration of tires for the C7.

Jim Mero puts the C7 through its paces as he evaluates the latest development in tires for the Stingray.

operation of the car's power top. At top speed, he noted, "there's a tremendous amount of force trying to peel the fabric off the top."

There also is the "max pothole" test. A 3.8-inch pothole is part of the GM proving ground test track. It slopes on one side but has vertical wall on the other.

"Driving into it at twenty-five miles per hour in a Corvette is like running over a curb," Holder said. "It feels like it's going to knock the fillings out of your head. Most Corvette customers would consider it an accident."

While the Corvette is not designed or certified to tow a trailer, "that doesn't stop people," Holder said, so the engineers install trailer hitches, hook up trailers, and pull them up hills in the hottest of weather conditions, all to test engines, transmissions, and final drives.

"The car has plenty of power," Holder said. "The biggest reason we don't offer towing is we're not going to add the mass or the space associated with a tow hitch."

Another extreme that perhaps only a minority of Corvette owners will encounter is tested in northern Canada. In the coldest regions, "most severe cold-weather customers would never think about [exposing their Corvettes]."

On the other hand, Corvette owners probably wouldn't be surprised by Mero's high-speed testing, or by what Holder terms the Woodward Test, named after Woodward Avenue, which runs from Detroit to Pontiac and has been the home of stoplight drag races since the days of the famed Detroit muscle cars.

For the Woodward Test, the throttle is held wide open, the transmission is set in third gear, and the clutch is dumped. "It sounds like a whole lot of fun, and it is—for the first couple of times," Holder said. "But we do it hundreds of times to make sure the powertrain and clutch and whole car is capable."

While the Corvette owner might do this to his or her own car from time to time, the engineers have to do it "over and over and over again, and without allowing the car to cool down, so we can see the instrumentation and gather the data."

Holder remarked that the bottom line of testing to such extremes—even testing to the breaking point—is "doing this so customers don't have to."

It's one thing to reveal a car with a beautiful body and interior, a car that looks fast even when it's just sitting there. But it's another thing to be able to assure buyers that their cars not only look fast, but are fast, and are not just fast, but dependable, durable, safe, and even fuel-efficient.

"There's a lot of pressure," on the development team, Holder said. "We unveiled the most exciting car a lot of people have seen in a long time, and we've made a lot of promises. Now we have to deliver on that promise, and it's not just sitting back and watching the chips fall into place. There are a lot of challenges to be overcome."

8 LAUNCH

How did General Motors tell the world a new Chevrolet Corvette was coming?

Very quietly, at least at first.

On May 4, 2011, General Motors issued a 580-word news release announcing the company's intention to invest $131 million in its assembly plant at Bowling Green, Kentucky, "to support production of the next generation Chevrolet Corvette." It was the first official confirmation of a seventh-generation Corvette.

The press release quoted GM North America President Mark Reuss, Kentucky Governor Steve Beshear, and United Auto Workers Vice President Joe Ashton, and it noted that some 250 new assembly plant jobs would be created. But there was precious little news in the release about the car those new employees, and the other members of UAW Local 2164, would be assembling.

CONTROL

To underscore that the new seventh-generation Corvette truly marks the start of a new generation of the American sports car, the traditional crossed-flags Corvette logo was re-designed once more, drawing from the proud history of its six other predecessors.

John Fitzpatrick is marketing manager for Chevrolet Performance Cars, which include the Camaro, the SS and the Corvette. In that role, he helped plan the Stingray's unveiling and sales launch.

But now everyone (or at least those who read the fine print on the business pages or regularly logged in to Corvette enthusiast blogs) knew that, indeed, there would be a seventh-generation Corvette. But that was all they knew, because GM immediately enclosed the car and all details of its design and development in a cone of silence at least as large as the bright yellow cone that towers over the National Corvette Museum.

That silence extended to off-the-record conversations, even after September of that year, when spy photos of Corvette mules were published, and even after November, when a website shared illustrations it claimed accurately showed the exterior design of the C7 Corvette. The ban held even a few months after that, when professional and amateur photographers captured IVER Corvettes on engineering development drives—though everything but windows, wheels, tires, and lights was well hidden beneath not only black-and-white pattered camouflage, but also matte-black material over the camouflage.

Meanwhile, Chevrolet and its dealers were launching the 2013 model year version of the Corvette, a car that officially celebrated the Corvette's 60th anniversary. From a marketing standpoint, you don't want to talk about your 2014 C7 model when you still have 2013 C6s to sell, and in five flavors: standard coupe and convertible, Grand Sport, Z06, ZR1, and 427 Convertible Collector Edition.

That doesn't mean, however, that planning wasn't well underway for the official reveal and launch of the C7 Stingray.

TRYING TO CREATE A BIG SENSATION

Responsibility for executing the marketing plan devised for the C7 Stingray falls to John Fitzpatrick, a former General Motors regional sales manager from upstate New York who joined the home-office staff in 2007. Fitzpatrick served as marketing manager for the rebirth of the Chevrolet Camaro, a car launched amid major media and consumer frenzy. In the new GM organizational structure that followed the corporation's relaunch, Fitzpatrick's duties expanded. He became marketing manager for Chevrolet Performance Cars, a group that included the Camaro, the Corvette (C6 and C7), and the Chevrolet SS, which at the time was still a secret project.

The subsequent expansion in duties for Fitzpatrick and his team came with additional challenges as well. No longer could the Corvette be sold only to traditional, faithful, and hard-core enthusiasts—the next-generation Corvette had to draw buyers from a new generation of consumers.

"The brand is very, very strong in the market," Fitzpatrick said, "probably the most recognized GM nameplate out there. But the issue is that, for a lot of people, it's not very high on the shopping list. We have a core group of enthusiasts who love the car and who will continue to buy the car."

The problem, however, is that that group is aging.

"Seventy-five percent are more than fifty-five years of age," Fitzpatrick said, "so we need a plan that starts attracting younger people and gets them engaged with the vehicle."

Many of those younger potential buyers got not only the first official glimpse of the (camouflaged) 2014 Stingray, but also the first chance to take the car on a virtual test drive, through the Gran Turismo 5 racing game for Sony Computer Entertainment's PlayStation 3 system.

PIXELATED POWER FOR A NEW GENERATION

The availability of a C7 Corvette for downloading to the game was announced in November 2012. Almost immediately, half a million people took advantage of the free download and got behind the steering wheel—or joystick—of a camouflaged Corvette. After the car was unveiled in January in Detroit, virtual versions of a Corvette prototype without camouflage were made available for download. When real Stingrays started rolling off the assembly line at Bowling Green, another virtual version was available for download.

Look closely. That's not a C7 Stingray prototype hurrying around a race track—it's the virtual image of the car that was made available through the Gran Turismo5 racing game through Sony's PlayStation3 system.

Kazunori Yamauchi, president of Sony's Polypony Digital and creator of the Gran Turismo game, watches as Mark Reuss, president of GM North America, drives a virtual C7 Stingray around a race track.

More than one thousand different vehicles are available in the Gran Turismo 5 garage, but the seventh-generation Corvette was the first to be included so early in its development process. Takuya Asano, director of the Gran Turismo Explore Studio, said it was therefore hidden beneath full covers.

Asano is a graduate of the famed Art Center College of Design in Pasadena, California. After college, he went to work at Nike, doing interior designs for Niketown retail stores. He later designed Nike eyewear, worked with the Nike+ group, and then joined the Nike Explore Group, a think tank–style team exploring ways to enhance Nike brand awareness.

When Asano heard that Kazunori Yamauchi, president of Sony's Polyphony Digital and creator of the Gran Turismo game, had been invited to visit Nike executives, Asano talked his way into the meeting by volunteering to serve as an unofficial interpreter.

"Something I learned at Nike is that personal relationships are very important," Asano said, adding that he and Yamauchi quickly established a good rapport and that Yamauchi eventually invited Asano to leave Oregon and to establish an Explore-style group at Polyphony Digital near Sony Computer Entertainment Group's U.S. headquarters near Los Angeles. It was through another friend that Asano was introduced to designers at General Motors and eventually to the C7 Corvette. "A mentor of mine who had been design director at Opel, Hideo Kodama, still had many friends at General Motors," Asano said.

Kodama introduced Asano to another Art Center graduate, Frank Saucedo, the chief designer at General Motors' advanced styling studio near Los Angeles. Asano and Saucedo met from time to time "for coffee, just to chat," Asano recalled. Eventually, those chats included potential projects involving both of their respective companies. Eventually, a meeting was arranged between Yamauchi and Ed Welburn, the head of General Motors global design.

Initially, only camouflaged versions of the Stingray were available to virtual drivers...

"The Corvette is coming," Asano said. "We know we cannot pass up that opportunity."

It was Asano who first suggested including a camouflaged Corvette as part of the Gran Turismo 5 video game. "I grew up liking cars," Asano said, "and at a very early age I was fascinated by 'scoop' photos in magazines." (What Asano knew as scoop photos are images known as spy photos in American car magazines—photos of test cars hidden beneath various camouflage covers.)

"People don't get to experience those camouflage or test cars, how they drive," Asano said.

Corporate liability restricts the driving of such cars to key development engineers and precious few other GM employees. But Asano saw an opportunity to let others have at least a virtual sample of that experience, and a potential marketing opportunity for Corvette as well. An agreement was reached, and a group from Polyphony Digital flew to Michigan, where they photographed and took measurements of a camouflaged C7 IVER car.

"Millions of photographs," Asano said, explaining that Polyphony Digital may take a hundred photos of a headlamp and the way it illuminates or turns off. The goal, he said, is to make the computer-generated image on the video screen look as realistic as possible.

Asano said that after the Corvette was included in Gran Turismo 5, a producer for a national news show studied the video screen and was convinced that what he was seeing was real video, not CG animation.

The secret, Asano said, and what really sets Polyphony Digital apart, is not just the amazing attention to vehicle detail, but also the way light is used to illuminate the images.

"That's why it looks so accurate," he said. "It's the lighting, and that's the philosophy of Gran Turismo."

... but after the actually 2014 Corvette was unveiled, the car without its camouflage was available to Gran Turismo 5 players.

Yamauchi and Reuss announced the availability of the camouflaged Corvette, and half a million people downloaded the vehicle. "That was a surprise," Asano said. "It was our first time to unveil a test mule car in the game. Personally, I was always fascinated with such cars, but we didn't know if our users would be passionate about them."

Once the Corvette was unveiled at the Detroit show, Gran Turismo 5 players were offered a version of the car with its camouflage removed. Asano said those vehicles officially are still considered prototypes, in part because they do not show the final version of the car's exhaust system. That final version—the production C7—was available for download at the same time Stingrays were rolling off the assembly line and into dealer showrooms.

By mid-April 2013, more than 1.6 million Gran Turismo 5 players had downloaded either the camouflaged or prototype version of the C7 Corvette. But the actual number of drivers was much higher, Asano said, because people invited their friends to drive.

CORVETTE COMES HOME

While the video game helped create an early buzz among nontraditional Corvette buyers, the official unveiling of the real car and the early sales plan were aimed at traditional Corvette enthusiasts.

Just a few weeks before the 2012 Los Angeles show, Chevrolet revealed details of the new, fifth-generation small-block V-8 engine that would debut in the new 2014 Stingray as the LT1, generating "an estimated 450 horsepower," making it the highest-performance engine ever offered in the basic version of a Corvette.

Traditionally, vehicles such as a new Corvette are unveiled at one of the major international auto shows—in Detroit, Frankfurt, Paris, Tokyo, Geneva, or, in recent years, at Shanghai. The other major American shows (Los Angeles, Chicago, and New York) are also favored venues for significant reveals.

The Corvette marketing team considered introducing the car at the Los Angeles show in November 2012. Southern California is America's largest new and especially *sports car* marketplace, and the L.A. show has been growing in international importance. However, the team realized that there likely was too much time between the L.A. show and the start of C7 production, and the onset of C7 sales, to truly capitalize on the excitement and momentum that would be generated by showing the car so soon.

The New York show also was considered, but if Los Angeles was too early, New York, with its traditional Easter-tied date, was too late.

"It was really Detroit that fit into the sweet spot," Fitzpatrick explained.

The North American International Auto Show in Detroit is not only one of the world's most important auto shows—drawing media from around the world and new-vehicle introductions from a global array of automakers—but it is staged just a couple of blocks from General Motors headquarters on the Detroit Riverfront. And, by a quirk of the calendar, the 2013 Detroit show, held each January, was scheduled for a week later than usual.

The auto show is held in Cobo Center, an exhibition hall where various automakers rent space for their displays. But to give the Corvette the coming-out party Chevrolet thought it deserved, the unveiling was held on the eve of the auto show's press preview, not at Cobo, but rather at the Russell Industrial Center, a structure originally built in the early twentieth century to house the Murray Manufacturing Co., an earlier supplier of auto bodies to Detroit automakers. A new facility, designed by famed architect Albert Kahn, had been built near the original, and the campus eventually housed not only auto body–producing equipment, but also several printing companies. In recent years, the 2.2-million-square-foot building has become a center for art and entertainment.

Chevrolet invited several thousand people to the Corvette Reveal, including news media personnel in town from around the world, Corvette enthusiasts from around the country, and GM employees. Another 150,000 people watched the event live on the Internet.

On the eve of the 2014 North American International Auto Show in downtown Detroit, Chevrolet unveiled the new C7 Stingray.

"It was a very unique venue and a very unique reveal," Fitzpatrick said, adding that "the thing we found amazing was that if we had been a cable television show that Sunday night, we would have been one of the top-five rated shows, and would have outdrawn ESPN2, MSNBC, and HGTV.

"The buzz and the [media] coverage generated were bigger than the buzz and the coverage of the reveals that followed us [on the Detroit show floor]," he added.

But there was no time to bask in the aftermath of the Corvette Reveal or the Detroit show display (which included Corvettes from all seven generations). Instead, Fitzpatrick, Welburn, and others from Chevrolet had to abbreviate their time at the show to fly to Scottsdale, Arizona, where the first new Stingray would be auctioned for sale.

"Barrett-Jackson [Auction Company] has a long history with us of doing very memorable auctions," Fitzpatrick said. "They sold the first ZR1 about five years earlier. The Barrett-Jackson auction is really becoming, in some ways, the mecca for really die-hard car enthusiasts. And not only do you have Barrett-Jackson there, but Russo and Steele and other high-end auctions are taking place at the same time in the area. It becomes a car cornucopia for enthusiasts. It doesn't necessarily

In addition to news media from around the world, many Corvette enthusiasts were invited to the official unveiling of the C7 Stingray.

target the new customer we have to attract, but it generates a lot of awareness."

And a lot of money, though in the case of the sale of the 2014 Corvette, that money went neither to Chevrolet nor to Barrett-Jackson. Instead, money generated from the sale went directly to the College for Creative Studies, the famed design school in Detroit.

Furthermore, the last bidder standing would not get the Corvette show car that crossed the auction block. They would instead have to wait until late summer, when the C7s began rolling off the assembly floor.

That final bidder was Rick Hendrick, a Chevrolet dealer and NASCAR stock-car racing team owner, who bid $1.05 million for the first Corvette. That car, of course, would be a C7 coupe, because as yet there had been no announcement about a C7 convertible.

But just a couple of weeks after the Detroit show, Chevrolet announced that the convertible version of the C7 would be unveiled soon. To underscore the fact that this new-generation Corvette was designed and engineered for worldwide distribution and driving, the unveiling of the cabriolet would take place in early March at the Geneva show in Switzerland.

After its webcast unveiling for invited guests, the C7 Stingray was showcased at the North American International Auto Show, with Mark Reuss introducing the new car and two of his historic predecessors, the original 1953 model (left) and the famed split-window coupe of 1963.

The auto show display at Detroit featured the C7 with each of the previous six Corvette generations.

(From left) Chief engineer Tadge Juechter, GM Design vice president Ed Welburn, senior vice president of product development Mary Barra, and Mark Reuss, president of GM North America, pose with the new Corvette at its first auto show appearance.

Just hours after the camouflage came off, the new Corvette was up for bidding at the Barrett-Jackson collector car auction in Scottsdale, Arizona.

The new Corvette was featured at the annual Amelia Island Concours d'Elegance on Florida's northeastern coast, where concours founder Bill Warner presented GM Design vice president Ed Welburn with a letter opener that originally had been a gift to Bill Mitchell, the GM Design director and father of the original Stingray.

Ed Welburn discusses the new Corvette during a presentation at Amelia Island, where he shared the lectern with Peter Brock, one of the designers who helped create the original split-window Stingray for 1963.

More than 800 Corvette enthusiasts got a special glimpse of the C7 at a reception on Amelia Island.

What's more, the first Stingray convertible for public sale would be offered for auction at Barrett-Jackson's collector car event in early April, in West Palm Beach, Florida, with proceeds going to the Barbara Ann Karmanos Cancer Institute.

The bidding was spirited and aggressive once more. And once more, Rick Hendrick was the high bidder, this time securing the first convertible available for public sale for a cool $1 million.

The new Corvette was in much demand, and not just among car collectors. Chevrolet was approached by officials of the 2013 Super Bowl about including a new Stingray in the halftime show in New Orleans. Instead, a 2014 Stingray will be presented to the game's most valuable player and Super Bowl champion, Baltimore Ravens quarterback Joe Flacco.

The 2014 Corvette made its Los Angeles debut early in March 2013, when the Petersen Automotive Museum hosted a Corvette 60th birthday party. Many Corvette designers and engineers, an engineer from the new small-block team, and a tire engineer from Michelin gave presentations during the four-day National Corvette Museum Bash in April 2013.

Other events were also held in anticipation of the car's arrival in Chevrolet dealerships across the country, including the first drives by the automotive press.

Joe Flacco, the quarterback for the Baltimore Ravens, poses with a C7 Corvette. He'll receive a C7 for being honored as the most valuable player in the National Football League's Super Bowl XLVII.

The 2014 Chevrolet Corvette convertible made its U.S. auto show debut in New York, where it shared the stage with other Chevrolet Performance vehicles, including the Chevrolet SS sedan and the Chevrolet Camaro Z28.

The 2014 Chevrolet Corvette served as the pace car for the 97th Indianapolis 500, where cars powered by Chevrolet engines swept the first four positions and seven of the top ten.

Former Indianapolis Colts quarterback Jim Harbaugh was back in town to drive the 2014 Indy 500 Corvette pace car. Harbaugh is head coach of the San Francisco 49ers of the National Football League and part-owner of an Indy Racing League team.

Though the exterior has changed, the spirit of the original Corvette remains intact.

CREATING BETTER DRIVERS

But while the prelaunch activities and early sales effort focused on the Corvette choir, plans were being made to showcase the Stingray as an aspirational automobile for a much wider range of sports car buyers, first in North America and then around the world.

"Our goal is to protect our core loyalists and to make sure they have access to the car, and to get their feedback," Fitzpatrick said. After that initial push, marketing plans would preach to a much larger congregation. Many people whom Chevrolet sees as potential Corvette buyers "see us as a pure muscle car," said Fitzpatrick, whose marketing team is challenged with showing those potential buyers that while the Stingray has plenty of muscle, it also is as nimble as any of those sports cars costing two or three times as much. The Stingray is also much more technologically sophisticated and far more fuel-efficient. "Fuel economy is part of the surprise-and-delight the Corvette can deliver," Fitzpatrick said, "but you don't know that until you get behind the wheel and experience it."

Fuel economy is just one of the things, he added, that cannot be explained in a 30-second television advertisement. "They have to experience it for themselves."

The goal is nothing less than a sea change in perceptions.

"When they see the Corvette, they have a preconception of what they think a Corvette is," Fitzpatrick said. "For a lot of people, they think of it just as that big, old, hulking V-8 that does great in a straight line, but you wouldn't want to really take it on a road course. You have to overcome that.

"The exterior design goes a long way toward doing this. It keeps the essence of Corvette but also gives a bolder, different look.

"And now people are going to get into the car and see all kinds of premium materials—the aluminum is aluminum, the carbon fiber is carbon fiber—and we're going to try to explain to them that this is much more technologically advanced, not only in chassis technology but in human-interface technology."

And how will this happen? At a series of ride-and-drive events staged in conjunction with lifestyle events.

"There are eight key cultural coastal centers [in the United States]," Fitzpatrick said, "on the east and west coasts, and those are really where the trends start. We're developing a process where we can get into those markets and get those people to experience the Corvette and really have some fun with it and realize that we have a very credible two-seat sports car that's just as good as anything else they can buy."

The challenge and the key, Fitzpatrick said, is simply to get them to climb behind the steering wheel—"to engage them so they can see the car and sit in the car and feel all the things we've done with the car, to have a firsthand drive."

And more than that, to be able to do back-to-back comparisons with the sports cars they think are the best in the world.

The anticipated result is that those who may be new to the Corvette, and especially this new, seventh-generation Stingray, will discover what Fitzpatrick says those who already own a Corvette already know, "that if they're buying a Corvette, the car will make them better drivers."

CHAPTER

9 ASSEMBLY

Dave Tatman remembers the aftermath of General Motors' announcement it would invest $131 million and hire another 250 people to build the seventh-generation Chevrolet Corvette at its assembly plant in Bowling Green, Kentucky.

"Within the next couple of months I was at the Governors Mansion for a black-tie night before the [Kentucky] Derby," said Tatman, the Bowling Green assembly plant manager. "My wife and I were standing in the line to greet the governor and his wife. But he [Kentucky Gov. Steve Beshear] comes across the room to me and gives me a big hug and says 'Dave, we had a lot of fun making that announcement, didn't we? But now listen, you're not thinking of running for governor are you, because you're the most popular guy in Kentucky right now'."

Tatman knew he really wasn't the most popular guy in the Bluegrass State. A 32-year GM veteran who had worked in 12 other manufacturing plants in various locations, Tatman knew politicians tended to speak in hyperbole. But Tatman also knew that it wasn't only Corvette owners who appreciate their cars and the lifestyle it delivers. Tatman knew the governor was right about one thing: The enormous impact a manufacturing facility, especially one that produces a popular and world-class product, can have not just on the local community around the plant but on the economy and even the emotional satisfaction and status of an entire state, or in Kentucky's case, an entire commonwealth.

REQUIRED

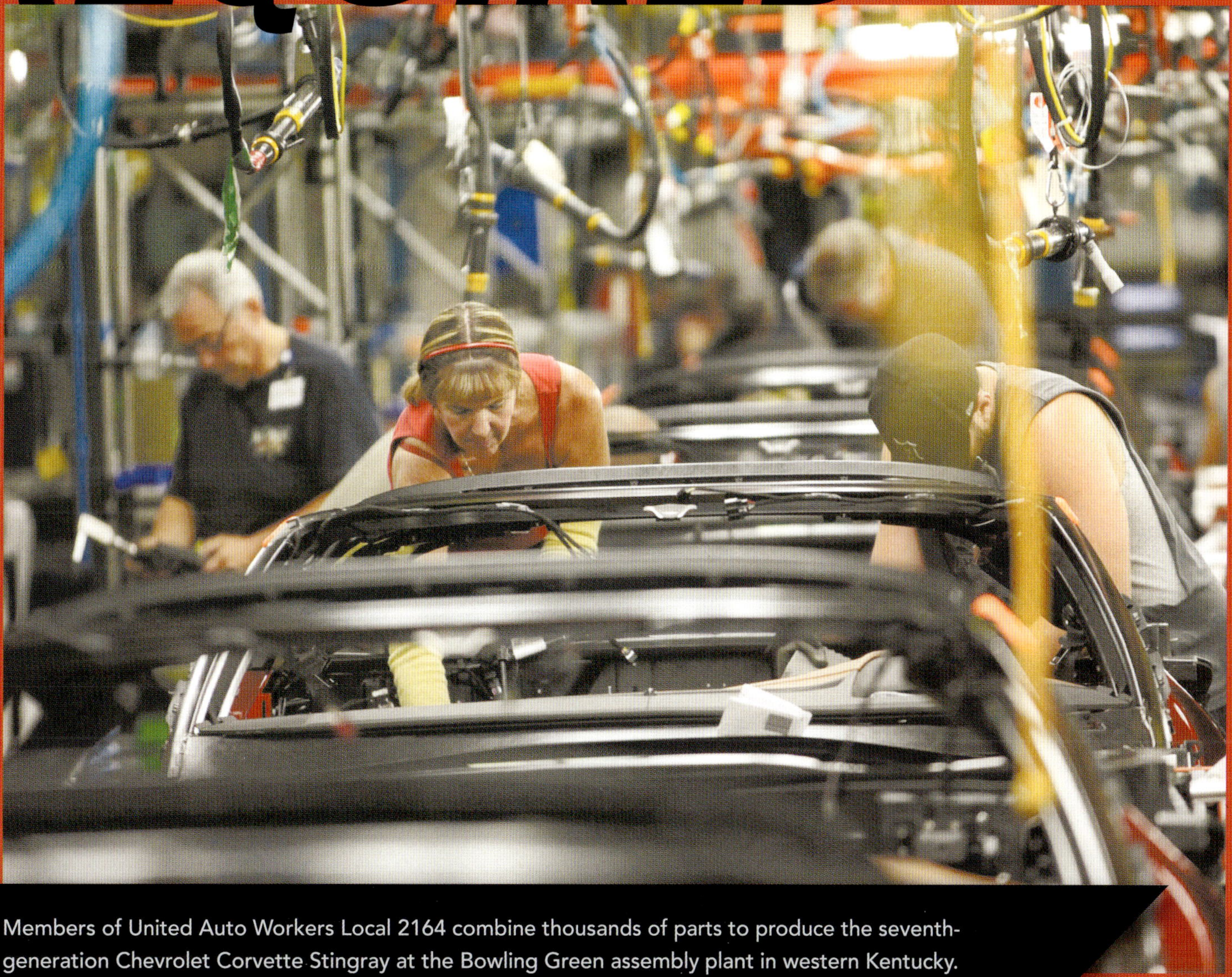

Members of United Auto Workers Local 2164 combine thousands of parts to produce the seventh-generation Chevrolet Corvette Stingray at the Bowling Green assembly plant in western Kentucky.

Robotic welders and other automated equipment handle heavy work with untiring precision.

Tatman also knew that the governor knew that the Bowling Green assembly plant's existence had been no sure thing. There was the issue of the General Motors bankruptcy, questions about whether the Corvette would stay in production, and if it did, whether GM would keep open a factory in which only one vehicle was built or would move that production to a more flexible and therefore a seemingly more efficient facility.

"There was a lot of concern in this area that the Corvette was going to die," Tatman realized as soon as he arrived at Bowling Green, his arrival coinciding with all the anxiety about whether the plant would remain on line.

For several years, the plant had built not only the Corvette but also the Cadillac XLR, a luxurious two-seater that shared its underpinnings and many of its parts with the Corvette.

But, Tatman said, the XLR became a casualty of the bankruptcy. "They simply stopped production," he said, and folks in Bowling Green knew that "if they stopped the XLR, what would stop them from eliminating the Corvette?"

But while Bowling Green lost a car, the lights were being turned off—and on a permanent basis—in 14 other General Motors manufacturing facilities.

Bowling Green had been building Corvettes for 30 years, and the National Corvette Museum was just across the street from the assembly plant, Tatman said, but the plant's future was no "slam dunk," he added.

The plant, the community, and the state would have to earn the right to remain the home of America's sports car.

And they did.

"There's a general recognition about the halo that goes with the Corvette," Tatman said. "And this area is recognized as the mecca for Corvette owners."

And not only by Corvette owners, but by those who wish they did. Bowling Green is one of the few automotive assembly plants in America that is open for public tours. "I've never had 50,000 people line up to watch me build transmission," Tatman said.

As the cars reach the start of the trim line, bins containing various components (the radio control module, antenna, rear vents, accelerator pedal, and more) are placed into the interior for each access and installation.

Chassis travel from the body and paint shops to the trim line, where wiring harnesses, instrument panels, doors, and other components will be added. Later, each chassis will be married to its powertrain and a seventh-generation Corvette will roll off the assembly line.

Each car is carried on a platform that has places, where the front fenders eventually will go, for bags to be hung. In those bags are components like window garnishes, front door brackets, and cooling ducts.

In a sub-assembly area next to the trim line, workers build up the instrument panels, which include the windshield headers.

In addition to the 50,000 people who tour the Bowling Green assembly plant each year, another 130,000 visit the National Corvette Museum across the street.

"A lot of the public has a vision of automotive factories that just aren't true today," Tatman added. "We take the responsibility [of public tours] seriously. It [a Bowling Green visit] may be someone's only view [inside the inner workings] of General Motors, and I think there's a lot to be said for opening our factories, and our foundries, which are not the fiery pits of hell. The floors are clean. What we've done in manufacturing is a story worth telling."

And worth seeing, and the community in western Kentucky only figures to have even more appeal for visitors with plans to build a racetrack-style motorsports park and test track just across the Interstate from the assembly plant and Corvette museum.

"Clearly, we had an edge," Tatman said. But it took a combined effort from from the statehouse to the factory floor to, as Tatman phrased it, "earn the right" to keep the Bowling Green assembly line in motion.

The announcement in the spring of 2011 that GM would invest in the tooling needed to build the seventh-generation Corvette, and would hire an additional 250 people to work with the nearly 600 already employed at Bowling Green assured everyone involved that the plant and UAW Local 2164 had, indeed, earned the right to stay in business.

"Now," said Tatman, "our responsibility is to build the finest sports car in the world."

JUST ANOTHER DAY AT THE OFFICE

Although the assembly line at Bowling Green wouldn't start rolling with new Stingrays until the third quarter of 2013, members of UAW Local 2164 actually started building seventh-generation Corvettes in 2011 when the first IVER cars were being constructed in a workshop near the General Motors Tech Center in Warren, Michigan.

"We've been very active in the launch cycles from the beginning," Tatman said, "with plant employees traveling to Detroit for more than two years. We identified a core launch team and they go to Detroit Monday-to-Thursday every week and work on the car side by side with the engineers and designers and technicians and others."

Bringing those who would produce cars on the assembly line into the process for building prototype vehicles not only helped the factory prepare for changes it would need to make — in some cases perhaps even inventing new tools and even new fastening systems in order to build a vehicle with such advanced technologies and materials — but alerted designers and engineers to potential obstacles that otherwise might not be encountered until cars were moving down the line in Bowling Green. Better to make changes before issues become problems.

Robotic arms assist human muscle to lift seats into position to go into the car.

A completed instrument panel moves via conveyor toward its installation in a C7 Stingray.

An engine is lowered into place on the front cradle, which already holds the front suspension.

The creation of a C7 Stingray starts in three separate areas of the Bowling Green assembly facility that stretches over one million square feet of structure set on 212 acres adjacent to Interstate 65 between Louisville and Nashville and not far from Mammoth Cave National Park.

In one area of the plant, a car's aluminum frame is created. In another, its body panels, made from SCM (Sheet Molded Compound) or carbon fiber and which have been delivered to Bowling Green by their supplier, are washed, primed and painted in sets. In yet another, the car's cockpit—which includes the windshield frame and completely wired instrument panel—is created. (In the paint shop, panels for several cars are painted in batches, along with a supply of spare panels. This is done so, should a fender or door skin be damaged before a car leaves the factory, a spare painted with the exact paint formula is available as a replacement.)

The aluminum used to build the Corvette's frame is made from carefully formed sections designed with specific rigidity and energy-absorbing properties. Three sub-assemblies—left- and right-side frame rails and a central "tunnel" section—are produced in specially designed cells by robotic laser welders. Various brackets also are welded in place as the separate frame sections move toward their eventual union.

The steering wheel is secured to the steering column hub.

A robotic arm helps move the radiator into place.

The rear hatch glass is carefully secured in place.

Rear quarter windows and molding are properly positioned.

Various welding technologies are employed for various parts of the frame, and welding temperatures are carefully controlled to maintain the metal's structural integrity, including welds; spot welds; MIG welds; flow-drill screws (as the screw is inserted, heat is generated that turns the aluminum molten—thus "flow"—but as soon as the proper torque is achieved, the aluminum immediately returns to its solid state); proprietary concentric welds (with 10 times as many bonds as might otherwise occur); even welds that are reinforced by special adhesives.

Conveyers carry left- and right-side frame rails to another cell where they are joined to a tunnel section. Bumper beams are added. The seat raiser, a structure behind the seats, is welded into place. So is the roof "bow" that is part of Stingray coupes.

When a frame is completed, it is carried by conveyor to a new area where it receives a special protective electrophoretic or E-coat treatment. The treated frames then return to the body shop section of the plant, where they are placed on orange "build bucks," automated carts with sensors that move via a guidance system attached to the factory floor.

Composite panels are attached to a car's frame—the rear tub section; the rear upper section (to which the rear hatch eventually will be secured); the floor pans; door ring; and wheel houses (to which fenders will be attached later in the process). Panels are attached with special adhesives applied with new adhesive dispersing technologies and applied in a process that controls temperatures and clamping times for optimized adhesion.

The cockpit is loaded into position and is secured with mechanical fasteners and adhesive bonding in a process that doubles the dimensional stability of the sixth-generation car, which is especially important for the C7 convertible.

A windshield is lowered into position.

While bodies are being trimmed out, suspension components have been built up on sub-frame.

The car now moves from the body shop to the general assembly area, where its body panel also have been delivered along with other parts specified by a vehicle's individual manifest in a system which allows the auto workers to focus on installation instead of running around finding parts.

Rear quarter panels are installed. Then the seats. Doors are added. Next, robots position the windshield. The fuel tank and other under-car parts are attached.

Then comes the "marriage ceremony" with the engine, transmission and differential wedded to the chassis.

The front and rear suspension sub-assemblies are installed and the engine is "dressed" as the bell housing, engine harness, starter, and motor mounts are installed. (The Corvette has several wiring harnesses. One is positioned within the frame early in the process. Others are added on the Trim and Chassis assembly lines.) Those that run through the underbody panels and those positioned toward the rear of the car are anchored by the use of "riv stud" fasteners, a special aluminum version of a steel rivet that provides significant weight savings on the C7.

Front fenders are attached, headlamps installed, and the hood put into place, as are the rear hatch and hatch glass and rear quarter windows.

A new sonic-welding technique is applied, using intense vibration to fuse the inner and outer parts of the front and rear fasciae, which are then installed.

Wheels, with their tires in place and aired up, are bolted on. Fluids are filled, the engine computer is flashed with its software, and the car is started. Various labels are attached, a final inspection is done, and the dealer-installed items are put into place—floor mats, owners manual, navigation system discs—so everything is ready for a dealer's service department to put into the car after it's come off the hauler and been cleaned for its new owner.

The car is driven off the line for additional inspections, including a trip through the DVT (dynamic vehicle test), a close look at painted surfaces, wheel alignment, and a trip through the hurricane-like water test booth. The car then goes outside, to the dynamic squeak and rattle test track.

Next, it's back inside to the factory car wash and then yet another and final inspection of the exterior and interior.

Dave Tatman remembers his first day at Bowling Green. In June, 2010, he was suffering through the demise of a GM transmission plant in Willow Run, Michigan. Tatman had started his GM career at Willow Run, when the plant had 13,000 employees. He'd returned to Willow Run in 2008 and found that "the wheels were coming off." Only 1,600 people still worked there, "but there were five million square feet of fixed costs." The plant closure was announced in the summer of 2009, "to my great disappointment, that was a dark day in my career." Instead of running a plant, Tatman's new job was to keep the plant closing from ruining lives by finding employees other jobs at other GM facilities.

Engines and transmissions are also being prepped to take their place on the sub-frame.

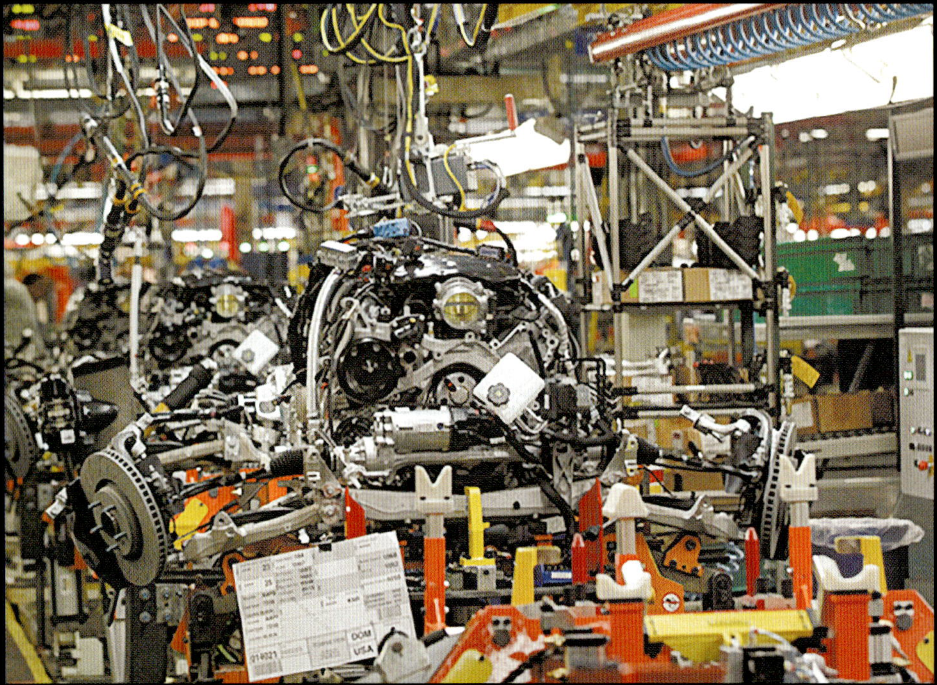

The completed powertrain and suspension sub-frames move toward their union with a C7 body.

FRONT

DOM
USA
M

A C7 body hovers over its powertrain and suspension as the "marriage ceremony" begins.

"We were working through that," Tatman said, when his own boss called him one Saturday moring, "and he would never call me on a Saturday."

"Do you own a Corvette?" Tatman's boss asked.

"No," Tatman responded.

"Do you like Corvettes?" the boss asked.

"I'm alive and breathing," said Tatman. "Of course I like Corvettes."

"Well, how would you like to build them?" the boss inquired.

"My first day, August 15, we delivered a new ZR1 to Brad Paisley, and he spent several hours with us," Tatman recalls. "Where do you go from here? A country music star thinks I'm a rock star!"

And Paisley wouldn't be the last person to ask Tatman for his autograph.

"I spent two hours at [Corvettes at] Carlisle this year just signing hoods for people," Tatman said.

"This job is like having two jobs. I have all the usual plant responsibilities, but I also have this significant role in the Corvette community and in the [Bowling Green] community. I live the car 365 days a year."

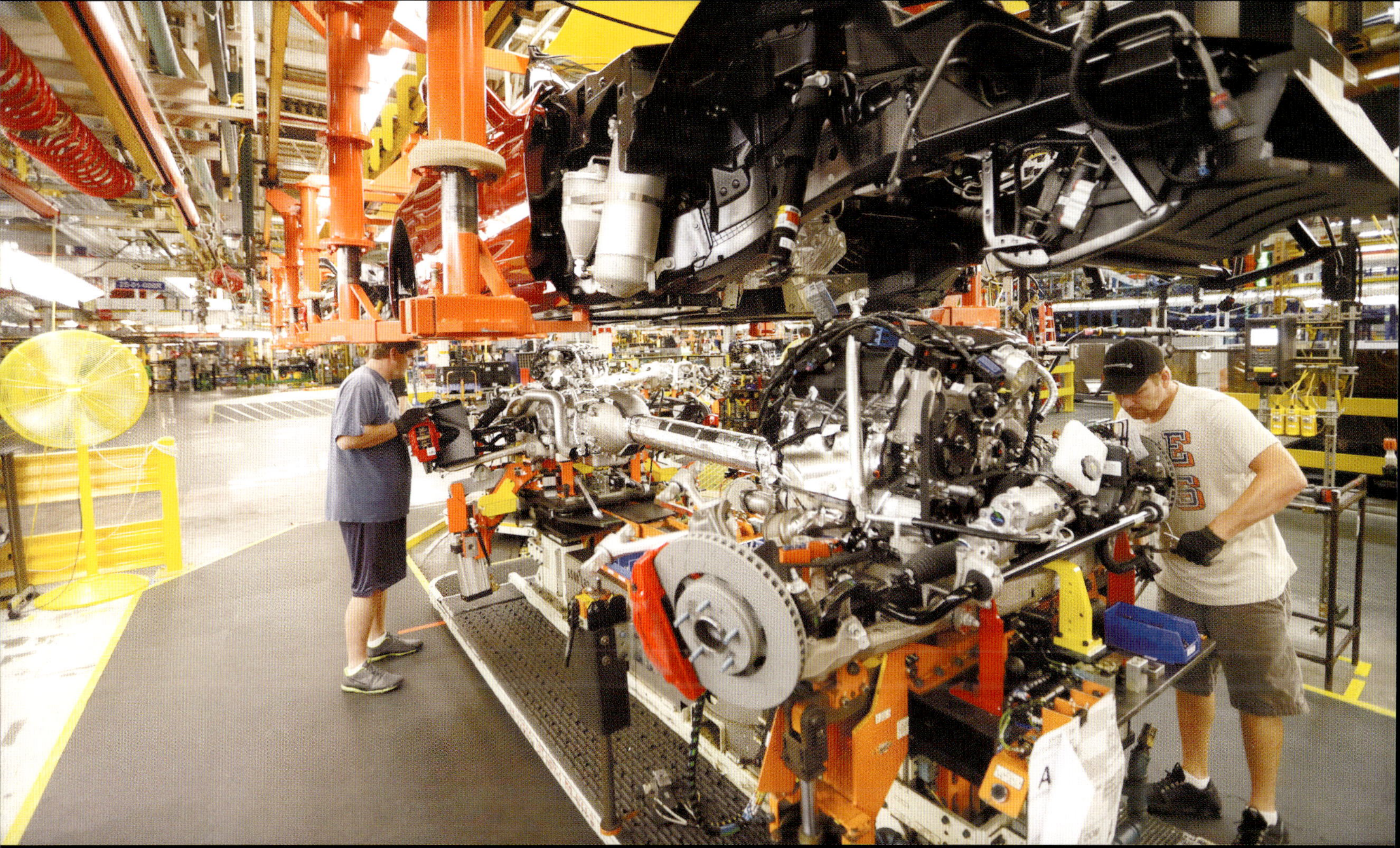

The body lowers into position and then is secured to the undercarriage.

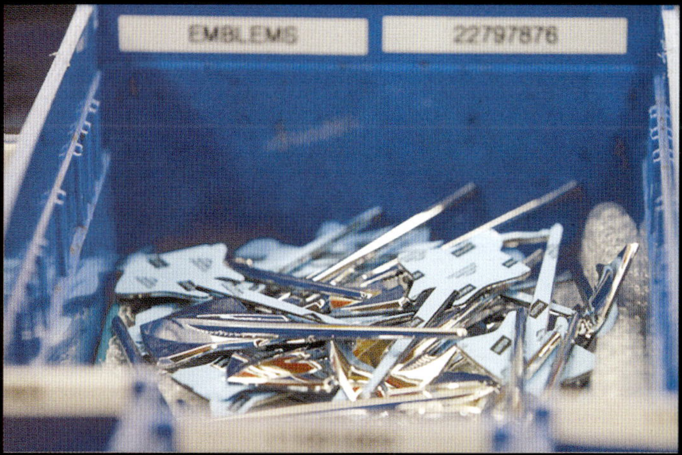

A template is used to make sure each Stingray emblem goes into the proper place on the new Corvette's front fenders.

Front fenders are secured in place.

Like other GM assembly plant managers, Tatman is on a first-name basis with seemingly everyone who works at Bowling Green, where the community atmosphere is so strong that many of the non-GM employees, people who work for suppliers, "want to be part of what we do, even asking to participate in our United Way campaign," and attending the monthly all-plant meeting Tatman hosts to keep employees and others informed on everything from opportunities to serve local charities to solving issues that might occur on the assembly line.

And it's not just the people who work at the plant who take things personally.

"There aren't many places wheres a customer call the plant manager" Tatman suggested.

"I make it a point to try to meet every customer who is in the plant to watch his car be built," he said.

Many of those customers take delivery of their vehicles at the museum. Although the museum is separate from the plant, Tatman boasts about the fact that so many former assembly plant employees now help with those customer deliveries at the museum, and added while those museum deliveries are scheduled through the buyer's local Chevrolet dealership, "the museum delivers more cars than any dealership in the country."

The Bowling Green assembly plant builds only a few thousand Corvettes each year. By contrast, a transmission plant may produce millions of gearboxes.

"But," Tatman said, "you don't have the end customer who looks you in the eye and says 'thanks for building my dream'."

All trimmed out, the cars moved via overhead conveyor to be married to their engine, transmission, suspension, and other components.

The post-assembly inspection includes many checks, including the headlights.

Completed cars are displayed next to the assembly plant sign adjacent to Interstate 65 in western Kentucky.

CHAPTER 10

DRIVING

For many people of a certain age, the dream of owning and driving a Corvette was ignited the moment they first saw the concept car at the Motorama show back in 1953. For others, it was triggered as soon as they eyed the roadster in their local Chevrolet dealership's showroom, or on the street, or at the races. For some of us, it was watching the *Route 66* television series, seeing Tod and Buz and their sporty little car and wanting to explore the country in a Corvette of our own. For others, it was seeing that first split-window, the 1963 Sting Ray 'Vette. For still others, it was later models, or watching the C6R at more recent races, or perhaps even getting to "drive" the newest Stingray in the video game *Gran Turismo 5* while the real-life car was still cloaked in camouflage.

And for some, it will be seeing the seventh-generation Corvette on the road for the first time.

But regardless of where or when, the dream of owning and driving a Chevrolet Corvette has become more than merely a popular fantasy. Over the course of several generations—both generations of people and generations of Corvettes—that dream of getting one's hands on America's sports car has become something of an American birthright, part of the fabric of the culture and embedded in our DNA.

THE DREAM

With up to 460 horsepower, but also achieving 29 miles per gallon on the highway, the seventh-generation Chevrolet Corvette Stingray is the ideal road trip vehicle for a driver and his or her best friend.

So what's it like when that dream becomes reality—when we actually get to drive this newest of Chevrolet Corvettes?

DEFINING NEW STANDARDS

"Refining Modern Performance" is the title of the brief slide show that Tadge Juechter, the Corvette's chief engineer, shares before the first drive of the new car.

"More technology: Enhance the experience when you want, easily turned off when you don't," reads the first slide. A follow-up slide notes that advanced technologies like the Drive Mode Selector, eLSD (electronic limited-slip differential), and Active Rev Matching are "designed to enhance, not distract from, the driving experience."

"More capability: Race proven aerodynamics; stronger, lighter structure; track-capable Z51," we continue reading. "Faster lap times than a Grand Sport, on smaller wheel/tire package."

You want fast? Check these numbers:

- 0–60 miles per hour in 3.8 seconds
- a quarter-mile sprint in 12 seconds, topping out at nearly 120 miles per hour
- 60–0 stopping within 107 feet
- cornering grip of 1.03*g* (and Juechter notes that this figure may get even better based on additional testing before the official start of production)

"More power and fuel economy: 460 hp / 465 lb-ft of torque, represents a 6 percent gain in output," the redefinition of the refinement continues. And yet, despite offering so much power, the new car also provides "better fuel economy than the 2013 Corvette."

By the way, that 2013 C6 Corvette was rated at 430 horsepower, 424 pound-feet of torque, and 16 miles per gallon in town or 26 on the highway. This new C7 Stingray is both more powerful and more efficient. Juechter and his team anticipate a highway fuel-economy rating of 29 miles per gallon.

But fuel economy isn't our first concern when we climb in behind the new Corvette's steering wheel. What we want, of course, is to feel the full force of 460 horsepower. Well, actually, we should say the full force of 455 horsepower. It seems only right that for our first drive of the C7 on public roads we drive the standard Stingray, not one with the Z51 track pack and its slightly less-restrictive exhaust system, which frees up that extra five horsepower.

In fact, the C7 we're driving carries no optional equipment. It's the basic—though it's difficult to describe it as any sort of "base"—model. This is the 2014 Chevrolet Corvette Stingray, introduced at the manufacturer's suggested retail price of $51,995, which includes seemingly everything you really need and then some: dual-zone automatic climate control; OnStar; touch-screen control for the Bose audio; Chevrolet MyLink, Bluetooth, and SiriusXM satellite radio; cup holders;

The C7 Stingray works for the daily commute to work, the weekend road trip, or when pushed all-out at the race track.

power and USB ports (and even an SD card slot); cruise control; power locks and windows; keyless entry and push-button starter; rear-view camera; GT seats with eight-way power adjustment; power-tilt and telescoping steering column; high-intensity discharge Xenon and LED headlamps; power and heated exterior mirrors; removable carbon-fiber roof . . .

The list goes on.

First impression: I'd driven maybe half a mile when I started thinking "Road trip!" and speculating about how much fun it would be to drive this car with its 455 horsepower and 7-speed rev-matched manual shifter on a long trip, especially one that included mountain grades and switchback turns where that rev-matched gearbox would really come into play.

Speaking of playing, I can't help but experiment with the Drive Model Selector, a dial on the center console just behind the gear-shift lever. Start the car and the selector defaults to the Tour mode. Twist it to the left and you engage the Eco mode for maximized fuel economy. Twist a little more to the left and you are ready for inclement weather. But if you're in Tour and you turn the knob to the right, you encounter the Sport mode, which not only tweaks the steering, throttle, gear-shift software, and even the tone of the exhaust, but also changes the display on the instrument panel to feature a huge tachometer with a "halo" that changes from white to yellow to red as you approach redline.

Turn the knob even further to the right and you enter Track mode, which provides more aggressive software settings and an instrument-panel display that looks as though it came right out of the C6R race car.

For now, however, we're still in break-in mode—putting mileage on the car while using all that this new Corvette has to offer—so I'll be content with the Tour and Sport modes as we learn and enjoy the drive.

One thing I discover is a touching, if unexpected, link between this newest Corvette and the very first Corvette. In 1953, the Corvette's tachometer included an odometer-style window that showed how many times the engine's crankshaft had turned; in other words, lifetime rpm. Well, one of the display screens available to the driver of the new Corvette shows not only lifetime rpm, but the number of hours the engine has been running since the car first came alive on the assembly line.

Here's another thing I learn: The fuel economy can be amazing for a sports car capable of speeds in the 190-mile-per-hour neighborhood. That's in part because the new Gen5 small-block V-8 that powers the new C7 Corvette Stingray is equipped with Active Fuel Management technology that, in low-load driving situations, allows it to operate as a 3.1-liter V-4 engine that pumps out 126 horsepower but a still-impressive 221 pound-feet of torque.

The figure of 126 horsepower may not sound like a lot, but consider that this new Corvette is so aerodynamically efficient that you need a mere 12 horsepower to keep it rolling down the highway at a rate of 50 miles per hour.

Consider as well that you won't even notice when the engine goes from eight to four cylinders, or that when it does, a barely discernible nudge to the accelerator pedal instantly reignites those other four cylinders and immediately puts the new small-block's full power at your disposal.

SMALL-BLOCK, BIG OUTPUT

To fully explore everything the new Gen5 small block V-8 and the new seventh-generation Chevrolet Corvette have to offer, however, we'll need to move from public roads to an autocross course or a purpose-built race track. We'll also need to equip our new Stingray with the Z51 Performance Package, which, for $2,800, adds high-performance gear ratios, transmission and differential coolers, ducts to cool the larger slotted brake rotors housed inside larger (19-inch front and

The Premiere edition of the 2014 Corvette bears the Stingray badge, its first appearance since 1976.

Looks can be deceiving: the seventh-generation Chevrolet Corvette Stingray is rated at 29 miles per gallon when cruising the highway, and it gets 30 miles per gallon when the driver opts for the "Eco" mode via the Drive Mode Selector.

20-inch rear) wheels and tires, and an electronic Limited Slip Differential (eLSD). Adding the Z51 Performance Package also lets us further equip the new Stingray with Magnetic Ride Control, an adaptive suspension system that enhances ride and handling on the road or the track, and Performance Traction Management, software designed to take full advantage of all performance systems, for an additional $1,795.

And to explore the car's full range of capabilities, we'll need driving skills to match. Oh, how the typical driver will be amazed at how much more proficient the car and its technology makes him or her.

For example, all new Stingrays equipped with manual transmissions come with Active Rev Matching technology, which blips the throttle (matching engine rpm from release of the clutch to activation of the clutch) for seamless shifting. It's a technique used on the racetrack, and on the street by really good drivers, who work the clutch with their left foot while manipulating the brake pedal with their right toes and the accelerator pedal with their right heel. But it takes a lot of practice to master. Unless, of course, you have a Stingray that matches the revs for you!

For another example, to demonstrate the eLSD, Corvette engineers set up an exercise in which we accelerate to 60 miles per hour, step off the accelerator pedal, and turn sharply to the right—at 60 miles per hour! The eLSD uses input from yaw, latitudinal, longitudinal, steering, and tire temperature sensors as well as the torque output from the engine to provide, accord to the eLSD overview, "optimal coupling torque to achieve driver's desired vehicle path and acceleration," whether on a wet road or a dry racetrack.

In our 60-mile-per-hour crank-the-wheel exercise, with eLSD turned off, the car fishtails wildly—a "tank-slapper," in racing terminology—or even spins out. With eLSD turned on, the car simply and calmly steers in a nice arc that the driver controls with the steering wheel. Why? Because the eLSD system has controlled the power being sent to each rear wheel to enhance vehicle traction and driver control.

But for most, the real awakening comes from sitting in the passenger's seat while an expert takes the wheel. In our case, that expert is Alex McDonald, C7 performance integration engineer—the man responsible for the integration of the Drive Mode Selector, steering, suspension and eLSD, as well as an accomplished sports car racer.

For the first media drive of the new Stingray, Chevrolet engineers have shared the autocross layout they use on the "Black Lake," a large, flat expanse of pavement at General Motors' Milford Proving Grounds northwest of Detroit, as well as the Milford Race Course, a purpose-built racing road course on that same property.

Autocrosses are racing events often held on empty parking lots and staged by various car clubs in which orange cones mark the driving course. Unlike in races on road courses or ovals, cars compete one at a time in autocrosses, with the winner determined based on the fastest time (minus penalties for striking any cones). In addition to local club events, there are national championships staged by official motorsports sanctioning bodies.

On a typical lap, the cones will mark an area for straightaway acceleration, often ending in a sweeping turn that leads into a slalom, followed by a couple of much tighter turns, a lane-change maneuver, and a hard-braking zone at the end of the lap. Each lap challenges the capabilities of both car and driver.

Because it is used for vehicle development, the autocross course on Milford's Black Lake is longer than most, therefore allowing vehicles to achieve higher speeds and higher load forces. I drive several laps as McDonald talks about the Drive Mode Selector, eLSD, and other features, and then we change seats so he can demonstrate their full—and fully awesome—capabilities.

Later, we head to the MRC, the full-blown racing circuit where the challenge involves even higher speeds, elevation changes, blind curves, and a daunting tall, tightly radiused turn nicknamed the "toilet bowl" because it's so steeply banked.

Here, again, the typical driver enjoys the way the car makes him or her a better driver and is simply awed by what someone with McDonald's skill can do behind the wheel.

We began this book by asking if it really matters who or what inspired the first Chevrolet Corvette. What really matters, however, is that the inspiration became a concept car which went into production and now, some 60 years and seven generations later, America's sports car is better than ever.

While the new C7 Stingray is built on tradition, it combines engineering excellence, advanced technologies, innovative design, and a determination not to simply meet but to exceed customer expectations.

The result is a car that achieves dynamic capabilities that previously seemed impossible to provide in a single vehicle: easy use with amazing fuel efficiency for the road, and awesome yet controlled performance that provides a genuine thrill ride on the race track.

Die-hard Corvette enthusiasts will love this car. But so will those who might be experiencing a Corvette for the first time, and even those who in the past may have been skeptical about an *American* sports car.

But now, with the launch of the C7 Stingray, the Chevrolet Corvette is more than just the American sports car; now, the Corvette is, quite truly, a world-class sports car built for the 21st century driving environment.

The 2014 Corvette Stingray is as functional as it is elegant. It is truly a groundbreaking automotive success.

APPENDIX CHARTS

MOST FUEL-EFFICIENT 450 HP CARS ON THE MARKET

Make	Configuration	HP	Torque	Highway MPG
Chevrolet Corvette Stingray	**6.2L V8**	**460**	**465**	**26+**
Porsche 911 Carrera S	3.8L H6	400	325	27
Audi RS5	4.2L V8	450	316	21
Mercedes C63 AMG	6.2L V8	451	443	19
Aston Martin DB9	5.9L V12	459	510	19
Jaguar F-Type S	5.0L V8	495	460	23
Audi R8 Coupe	5.2L V10	525	391	19
Nissan GT-R	3.8L V6	545	463	23
Lamborghini Gallardo	5.2L V10	550	397	20
Lexus LF-A	5.0L V10	552	354	16
BMW M5	4.4L V8	560	500	20
Ferrari 458 Italia	4.5L V8	562	398	17
Mercedes SLS AMG	6.2L V8	563	479	20
McLaren MP4	3.8L V8	616	443	22

The Corvette Stingray features the LT1, the fifth generation of Chevrolet's signature small-block engine. GM intended to push the limits of what this engine could do, and it has performed above and beyond their wildest expectations. Achieving 450 horsepower and also 450 pound-feet of torque, the new Corvette Stingray isn't just fast, it's also extremely efficient. New technology reduces cold-start emissions up to 25%, and the Active Fuel Management system allows the small-block V-8 to effectively turn into fuel-efficient V-4 in low-load driving situations, such as cruising along the freeway.

According to Sam Winegarden, GM vice president of global engineering, the LT1 represents "the most significant redesign in the small-block's nearly 60-year history." "The LT1," he continues, "is a sweetheart of a power plant, and drivers will feel its tremendous torque and power at every notch on the tachometer."

STRATEGIC USE OF INNOVATIVE MATERIALS

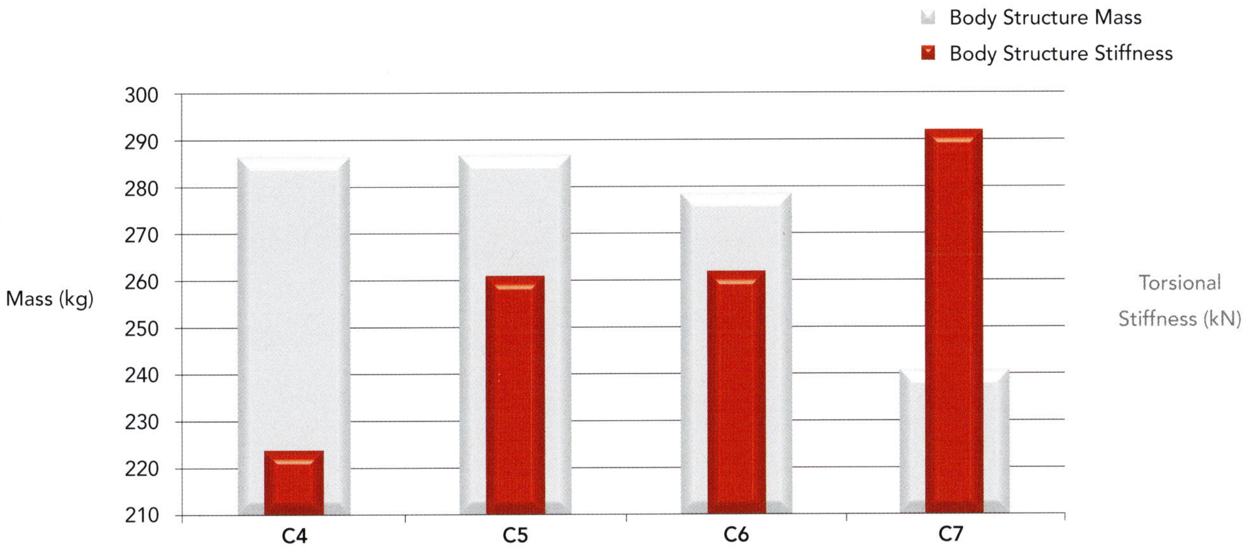

The new Corvette Stingray represents another huge leap forward for GM engineering. As the weight of the Corvette continues to decline, more imaginative and exciting materials make the vehicle stronger and lighter than ever, ensuring safer, more fuel-efficient rides for Corvette drivers everywhere. From aluminum alloys to heat-sensitive morphing metal technology, the new Corvette Stingray features futuristic design in a classy, contemporary package. In short, every aspect of the new Corvette—from its streamlined exterior to its racing-inspired interior—combine for a driving experience like no other.

LT1 V-8 LINE CHART

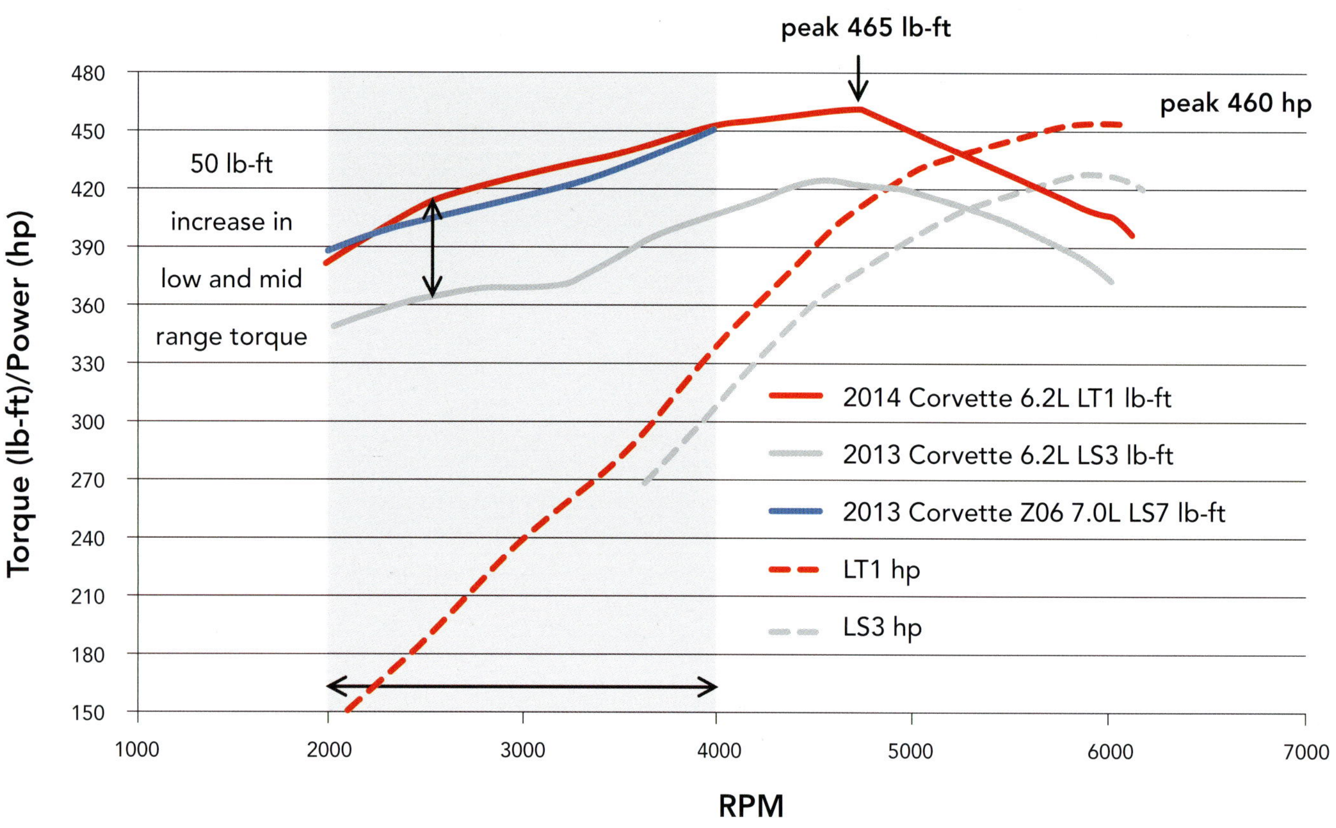

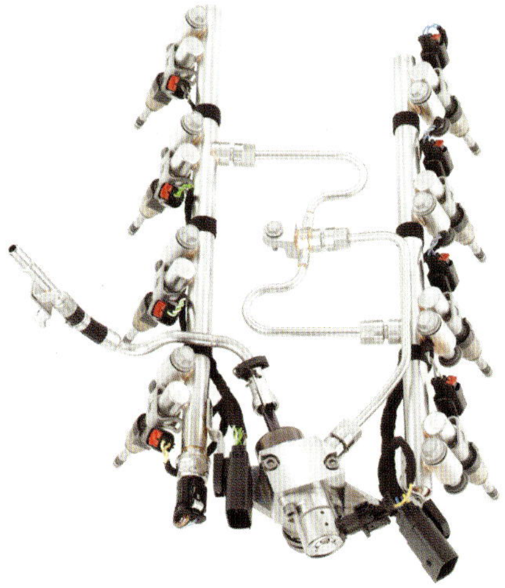

In 1955, the original small-block produced 195 horsepower from a modest 4.3 liters. The new 6.2L V-8 makes 450. Jordan Lee, global chief engineer and program manager for the small-block, calls the new engine "the most revolutionary change of the small-block in its 57-year history…this means exceptional power, torque, fuel efficiency, durability, and very low noise."

The new engine is optimized to provide the proper power and aural spectrums from idle to top speed in a wide variety of settings, meeting the demands of Corvette consumers from all grades of road across the country. Powertrain engineers were able to increase the engine's internal compression ratio, improving torque, efficiency, and power, without requiring drivers to buy premium-grade fuel. Over six million hours of computational time were spent on the combustion system alone.

Aluminum alloy keeps the new engines light but strong, and pressure-actuated oil jets spray the bottom of each piston and the surrounding cylinder walls to enhance performance at start-up and high engine speeds.

For even better results on the road, the Z51 Performance Package includes the eLSD, or electronic Limited Slip Differential, a program that optimizes traction depending on the road situation. One Corvette engineer described it like having one diff as you enter a corner, another at the apex, and a third at the exit of the turn. All together, the new LT1 can achieve 0-60 mph in 3.8 seconds; a quarter-mile jump in 12 seconds, maxing out at almost 120 mph; and an impressive 60-0 mph stopping ability within 107 feet. All in all, it's a pretty sweet package.

SPECIFICATIONS

2014 CHEVROLET CORVETTE STINGRAY

OVERVIEW

Model:	Chevrolet Corvette Stingray
Body styles / driveline:	2-door hatchback coupe with removable roof panel or 2-door convertible; rear-wheel drive
Construction:	composite and carbon-fiber body panels, hydro-formed aluminum frame with aluminum and magnesium structural and chassis components
Manufacturing location:	Bowling Green, Ky.

ENGINE

	LT1 6.2L V-8
Displacement (cu in / cc):	376 / 6162
Bore & stroke (in / mm):	4.06 x 3.62 / 103.25 x 92
Block material:	cast aluminum
Cylinder head material:	cast aluminum
Valvetrain:	overhead valve, two valves per cylinder
Fuel delivery:	direct injection
Lubrication system:	wet sump (Stingray) dry sump (Stingray with Z51)
Compression ratio:	11.5:1
Horsepower / kW:	455 / 339
Torque (lb-ft / Nm):	460 / 624
Recommended fuel:	premium recommended, not required
Estimated fuel economy (city / hwy):	17 / 29

TRANSMISSIONS

	Tremec TR6070	Tremec TR6070 – with Z51 Performance Pkg.	Hydra-Matic 6L80
Type:	seven-speed manual with Active Rev Match	seven-speed manual with Active Rev Match	six-speed paddle-shift automatic
Gear ratios (:1)			
First:	2.66	2.97	4.03
Second:	1.78	2.07	2.36
Third:	1.30	1.43	1.53
Fourth:	1.00	1.00	1.15
Fifth:	0.74	0.71	0.85
Sixth:	0.50	0.57	0.67
Seventh:	0.42	0.48	N/A
Reverse:	2.90	2.90	3.06
Final drive ratio:	3.42	3.42	2.56 (2.73 w/ Z51)

CHASSIS/SUSPENSION

Front:	short/long arm (SLA) double wishbone, cast aluminum upper and lower control arms, transverse-mounted composite spring, monotube shock absorber
Rear:	short/long arm (SLA) double wishbone, cast aluminum upper and lower control arms, transverse-mounted composite spring, monotube shock absorber
Active handling:	Magnetic Selective Ride Control (avail. with Z51)
Traction control:	StabiliTrak electronic stability control

BRAKES

Type:	front and rear power-assisted discs with four-piston fixed front and rear calipers (slotted rotors with Z51)
Rotor diameter (in / mm):	front: 12.6 / 320 (13.6 / 345 with Z51) rear: 13.3 / 338

BIBLIOGRAPHY

BOOKS

A Century of Automotive Style: 100 Years of American Car Design. By Michael Lamm and Dave Hollis, Lamm-Morada Publishing Co. Inc., Stockton, California, 1996

Camaro: A Legend Reborn. By Larry Edsall, Motorbooks, Minneapolis. 2009

Concept Cars: From the 1930s to the Present. By Larry Edsall, White Star Publishers, Vercelli, Italy, 2003

Corvette: America's Sports Car -- Yesterday. Today. Tomorrow. By Jerry Burton, Universe Publishing, New York, 2008

Corvette Racing: The Complete Competition History from Sebring to Le Mans. By David Kimble. Motorbooks, Minneapolis, 2012

Corvette: Sixty Years. By Randy Leffingwell, Motorbooks, Minneapolis, 2012

Corvette: The Shape of Performance, By the Auto Editors of Consumer Guide, Publications International, Ltd., Lincolnwood, Illinois, 2007

GM's Motorama: The Glamorous Show Cars of a Cultural Phenomenon. By David W. Temple, MBI Publishing Col., St. Paul, Minnesota, 2006

Legendary Cars: Cars That Made History from the Early Days to the 21st Century. By Larry Edsall, White Star PUblishers, Vercelli, Italy, 2005

Masters of Car Design, by Larry Edsall, White Star Publishers, Vercelli, Italy, 2008

Mike Yager's Corvette Bible. By Mike Yager, Krause Publications, Iola, Wisconsin, 2007

Overhaul: An Insider's Account of the Obama Administration's Emergency Rescue of the Auto Industry. By Steve Rattner, HoughtonMifflin Harcourt, Boston / New York, 2010

Standard Catalog of American Cars. Kruse Publications, Iola, Wisconsin, 1997

The Complete Book of Corvette: Every Model Since 1953, by Mike Mueller, Motorbooks, St. Paul, Minnesota, 2006

The GM Motorama: Dream Cars of the Fifties. By Bruce Berghoff. Motorbooks, St. Paul, Minnesota, 1995.

PERIODICALS

GM: Plans to include Corvette Stingray in Super Bowl halftime show scrapped. By Melissa Burden, The Detroit News, February 5, 2013

Higher-volume cars get carbon fiber. By David Sedgwick. Automotive News. March 18, 2013

WEB ARTICLES AND WEBSITES

1953 Corvette, By the Auto Editors of Consumer Guide, auto.howstuffworks.com

Vehicles carry messages at Chicago show, Larry Edsall's blog, iZoom.com, February 1, 2009

www.corvetteblogger.com

www.jalopnik.com

www.ricdetroit.org

ACKNOWLEDGMENTS

The author has many people to thank for their help in the execution of this book chronicling the design, development, and production of the seventh-generation Chevrolet Corvette.

Primary among them are Pete Martin and Jordan Wiklund. Pete works for Mullen, a public relations agency that helped General Motors on the Corvette launch program, and, along with Monte Doran of Chevrolet's communications staff, arranged many of the interviews I did and chased down much of the photography that appears in this book. Jordan is an editor and project manager at Motorbooks, the book's publisher, and for its parent, Quayside Publishing, and was a patient and understanding ear throughout the author's angst.

In addition to Monte and Pete, other key contacts for the author within the General Motors communications department or its associated agencies included Andrea Hales, Kari Nattrass, Jennifer Ecclestone, Michael Albano, Tom Read, Mary Ann Brown, Ron Ellis, Julie Esmer, Jim Brumfield, Andrea Lucido, Christina Abney, Emily Carter, Mallory Chaney, and Amanda Koons, as well as Katie Frassinelli of the National Corvette Museum.

Among those willing to be interviewed for this book were Tadge Juechter, Ed Moss, Josh Holder, John Bednarchik, Mike Bailey, Paul Alexander, Jim Mero, Alex McDonald, Peter Ho, Jason Kolk, Heath Holbrook, Harlan Charles, John Fitzpatrick, Ed Welburn, Tom Peters, Kirk Bennion, Hwasup Lee, Ryan Vaughan, Dave Tatman, Maren Taylor, and Doug Fehan. John Spencer and Bill Starr were not only interviewed, but also provided a guided tour of the Bowling Green assembly plant.

Photography was provided from several GM employee and staff photographers.

Also playing important roles in the production of this book were Brenda Eitelman of GM Licensing, Todd Christensen of the Chevrolet Division, Charles Robertson of Equity Management Inc., and Zack Miller, Madeleine Vasaly, and Nicole Schiele of Motorbooks.

Automotive photographer Brenda Priddy provided needed background information and Corvette expert and author Jerry Burton provided much needed morale support.

INDEX

Active Fuel Management, 88, 95, 102, 176, 182
Active Hatch Vent, 70, 72–73, 74, 90
Active Rev Match technology, 65, 89–90, 172, 174, 179
Aerogel insulation, 58
Akerson, Dan, 43
Alexander, Paul, 72–73
Aliyu, Jelani, 47
Amelia Island Concours d'Elegance, 146
American Le Mans GT1 championship, 26
Arkus-Duntov, Zora, 6, 13, 14–15, 16, 24, 26, 40–41, 45
Asano, Takuya, 138–140
Ashton, Joe, 134
Aston Martin, 24
  DB9, 182
  DBR1, 68
Audi
  R8, 64
  R8 Coupe, 182
  RS5, 182

Bailey, Mike, 83, 85
Barbara Ann Karmanos Cancer Institute, 147
Barra, Mary, 100, 102, 145
Barrett-Jackson Auction Company, 142–143, 145, 147
Bay, Michael, 37
Bednarchik, John, 80, 81
Belgian Block Road, 131
Bennion, Kirk, 23, 30, 33, 36, 38–39, 42, 43, 44, 45, 46–47, 48, 56, 58, 83
Beshear, Steve, 134, 152
Bilstein shocks, 126
Blue Flame, 12, 95
Bluetooth, 174
BMW M5, 182
Bohnstedt, Duane "Sparky," 10
Bose audio, 174
Brembo brakes, 83
Brock, Peter, 14, 146
Bruckheimer, Jerry, 37
Bugatti 57SC Atlantic, 14
Buick, 11, 33
  Encore, 43
  LaCrosse, 56
  LeSabre, 8, 9

C3, 16
C4, 16, 38, 121
C5, 6, 7, 16, 24, 30, 52, 74, 76, 96, 110
C5-R, 25
C6, 6, 7, 16, 20, 21, 25, 26, 29, 52, 55, 56, 58, 74, 76, 81, 83, 85, 88, 97, 106, 110, 115, 117, 119, 121–122, 124, 126, 127, 136, 174
C6R, 25, 27, 64, 78, 88, 170, 176
GT2, 25, 27
C6.5, 21, 33, 38
C7R, 28, 29
Cadillac, 11, 33, 43, 95
  ATS, 106
  XLR, 154
Charles, Harlan, 20, 23, 86, 87–88, 89
Chevrolet
  Camaro, 37, 38, 44, 110, 136
  Camaro Z28, 147
  Cobalt, 85
  Corvair, 13
  Corvette SS, 14–15, 43, 45, 136, 147
  Malibu, 56, 106
  Motor and Axle Plant, 106
  MyLink, 174
  Performance Cars, 136, 147
  Trax, 43
  Volt, 81
Chicago auto show, 37, 38
Chrysler, 18, 81
Church, John, 126
"Climb to the Clouds" race, 95
Cobo Center, 141
Cole, Ed, 10, 11, 12, 13, 95
College for Creative Studies, 143
Collier, Miles and Sam, 40
concept cars, 31–32, 45, 56
Corvette Museum and Hall of Fame, 82
Corvette Racing, 6–7, 25, 68, 69, 70, 77, 83, 86, 121
Corvette Reveal, 141–142
Cunningham, Briggs, 8, 68
Curtice, Harlow, 10

Daytona, 24 Hours of, 28, 29
Daytona Beach, 14, 24, 95
Detroit auto show. *See* North American International Auto Show
Driver Mode Selector, 86, 87–88, 89, 90, 174, 176, 178, 179, 180
DVT (dynamic vehicle test), 163

Earl, Harley, 8, 9, 10, 11–12, 14, 40
Ecotech engines, 106
Electronic Limited Slip Differential, 84
Electronic Throttle Control, 88
eLSD (electronic limited-slip differential), 85, 88, 126, 172, 174, 179, 180, 185
Emsley, Helen, 55
Engine Build Experience program, 106
EX-122, 10

Fehan, Doug, 24–25, 26, 28, 29
Fellows, Ron, 6–7
Ferrari, 24, 26, 68, 95
  458 Italia, 182

Finos, Dennis, 38
Fishel, Herb, 24
Fitch, John, 24, 68
Fitzpatrick, John, 136–137, 141, 142, 150–151
Flacco, Joe, 147
Ford Thunderbird, 13
Formula Ford, 119
Formula Vee, 119

G6, 56
Gen5 Small-Block V-8, 92–95, 96, 97–98, 99–100, 101–102, 103, 104, 105, 106, 107, 118, 141, 176
General Motors
  Advanced Design Studio, 37
  Global Design, 38
  Heritage Center, 43
  Motorama, 10–11
  Performance Division, 43
  Performance Vehicle studio, 44
  Powertrain, 96, 97–98, 102–103, 106
  Technical Center, 14, 30, 49, 110, 111, 157
General Motors Design, 8, 9, 17, 30, 33–35, 40, 43, 47, 49, 53–54, 55–57, 71
Special Anniversary Corvette Z06, 25
Generation-3 Magnetic Ride Control system, 84–85
GMC, 33, 106
  TerraCross, 43
Goodyear, 26, 121–122
  Gen-2 Z06 tires, 122
Gran Turismo 5, 136, 138–140, 170
Grand Sport, 14, 85, 110, 122, 131
Grossman, Bob, 24, 68

Hansgen, Walt, 24
Harbaugh, Jim, 149
Hendrick, Rick, 143, 147
Hill, Dave, 24, 25
Holder, Josh, 108, 110, 112, 114–115, 119, 130, 131–133
Holls, Dave, 8
Hotchkiss drivetrain, 11
hydroforming, 74

IMSA, 24
Indianapolis 500, 68, 95, 148
Indy Racing League, 149
IVER (Integration Vehicle Engineering Release), 109, 110–115, 120–121, 123–124, 126, 131, 136, 139, 157

Jaguar, 24
  F-Type S, 182
  XK-120, 95
  XK120, 8, 10
Juechter, Tadge, 18, 19, 20–21, 23–24, 25, 26–27, 28, 58, 68, 70–71, 74, 76–79, 82, 83, 84, 85, 86, 90, 92, 97, 98, 100, 107, 123, 145, 174

Kahn, Albert, 106, 141
Keating, Thomas, 10
Kimble, David, 26
Kodama, Hideo, 138

Laguna Seca, 25, 89
Lamborghini Gallardo, 182
Lamm, Michael, 8
Laurens Proving Grounds, 124, 128
Lauve, Henry, 10
Le Mans, 24 Hours of, 6–7, 22, 24, 25, 27, 28, 39, 40, 68, 70, 119
Lee, Hwasup, 43–47
Lee, Jordan, 92, 95, 97–99, 103–104, 106, 185
LeMay, Curtis, 8
Lexus LF-A, 182
Los Angeles auto show, 141
LS3 piston, 101
LT1 piston, 101
LT1 small-block V-8, 124, 182, 185
Ludvigsen, Karl, 14
Lutz, Bob, 128

MacKichan, Clare, 11
Magnetic Ride Control, 84–85, 87, 88, 126, 179
Mako Sharks, 16
Manta Ray, 45
Manufacturing Validation Build C7s, 119
McDonald, Alex, 85, 88, 119, 179, 180
McLaren MP4, 182
McLean, Robert, 10, 11–12
Mercedes
  C63 AMG, 182
  SLS AMG, 182
Mero, Jim, 119, 121–122, 124, 126, 128, 130, 131, 132
MG-TD, 8
Michelin, 7, 26, 88, 109, 121–122, 124, 131
  Pilot Sport Cup, 126
  Pilot Sport PS2, 126
  Pilot Super Sport, 83
Midcentury Motorama, 11, 12–13, 170
Middlebrook, John, 25
Milford Proving Grounds, 126, 129, 179–180
Milford Road Course (MRC), 126, 128, 179, 180
Mitchell, Bill, 14, 17, 24, 40, 146
Molde Fiber Glass Companies, 82
Montgomery, Scott, 131
Morrison, Robert, 82
Mosher, Jeff, 121, 124, 126
Moss, Ed, 74, 76
Mueller, Mike, 8

NACA ducts, 27, 78
National Corvette Museum, 8, 106, 113, 136, 147, 154, 156
  Motorsports Park, 106
National Football League, 147, 149
National Geographic, 28
Neal, Mike, 128
Nissan, GT-R, 182
Nomad, 13
Nordschliefe, 130
North American International Auto Show, 46, 56, 140, 141–142, 143–144
Northstar, 98
Nurburgring, 119, 130

Obama, Barack, 18
Oldsmobile, Aurora V-8, 24
Olley, Maurice, 11, 12
OnStar, 174

Paisley, Brad, 166
Parkinson, Ken, 123
Performance Traction Management, 87, 88, 179
Peters, Tom, 23, 38–39, 43, 44, 45–46, 48, 50, 52
Petersen Automotive Museum, 147
Petrucci, Mike, 88
Pikes Peak, 95
PlayStation 3, 136
Pohlmann, Chuck, 14
Polypony Digital, 138, 139
Pontiac, 33
Porsche, 68
  911 Carrera S, 182
Positive Crankcase Ventilation system, 103
Powerglide automatic transmission, 12
Pratt & Miller, 6, 24, 25, 78
Project Opel, 10, 11

Quad 4, 98

Renner, Carl, 10
Reuss, Mark, 43, 134, 138, 140, 143, 145
Road Atlanta, 128
Rolls-Royce, 11
Russell Industrial Center, 141
Ryan, Joe, 128
Rydzewski, John, 97

Saarinen, 14
Saturn Aura, 56
Saucedo, Frank, 138
SCCA national championship, 40
Schemansky, Joe, 10
Scott, Myron, 12
Sebring, 24
Sheet Molded Compound (SMC), 158
Shinoda, Larry, 14, 40
Sideswipe, 31–32, 37
SiriusXM satellite radio, 174
SMC (Sheet Molded Compound), 158
Sony Computer Entertainment, 136, 138
Spencer, John, 123
Spielberg, Steven, 37
Sports Car Club of America, 24, 40
StabiliTrak, 88
Super Bowl XLVII, 147

Tatman, Dave, 152, 154–155, 156, 163, 166, 168
Team Auto, 18, 20
Temple, David, 8
Thompson, Dick, 14, 40
Tire Temperature System, 88–89
Trans-Am Series, 24
Transformers, 31–32, 37–38
Transportation Unlimited, 11
Turin auto show, 14

United Auto Workers, 110, 112, 134, 153, 156–157
U.S. Department of the Treasury, 18, 33

Vaughan, Ryan, 36, 55–60, 61, 63, 64–65, 67
Virginia International Raceway (VIR), 122, 124, 128

Waldorf Astoria Hotel, 10, 12
Wallace, Tom, 25
Warner, Bill, 146
Watkins, Glen, 8
Welburn, Ed, 24, 33, 38, 41, 43, 45–46, 51, 55, 56, 57, 60, 138, 142, 145, 146
Willard, Lee, 126
Winegarden, Sam, 103, 182
Woodward Test, 132

Y1XX project, 19, 21, 23
Yamauchi, Kazunori, 138, 140

Z06, 7, 16–17, 25, 26, 76, 122
Z06 brakes, 122
Z51 Performance Package, 84, 122, 131, 172, 174, 176, 179, 185
ZL1, 44
ZR1, 7, 16, 26, 76, 119, 126, 166